LANNY

LANNY

BY LANNY McDONALD
WITH STEVE SIMMONS

FAWCETT CREST
TORONTO

A Fawcett Crest Book
Published by Random House of Canada Limited

ISBN: 0-449-21689-6

This edition published by arrangement with
McGraw-Hill Ryerson

COVER PHOTOGRAPH: Jim Allen
COVER DESIGN: Brant Cowie / ArtPlus Limited

Printed in Canada

First Fawcett Crest Edition: October 1988

To Ardell Mary, the lady who has made all my dreams come true. "Remember." – L.K.M.

CONTENTS

ACKNOWLEDGEMENTS

Writing this book has been fun, but it's also been hard work. There are a number of people who helped make this book a reality. My heartfelt appreciation goes to:

Mike Barnett of CorpSport International, who put the project together and gave me great advice throughout;

Mike Roy and Denise Schon of McGraw-Hill Ryerson, who wondered, I'm sure, if we'd ever mail that final chapter;

My mom and dad, who kept terrific scrapbooks of all those years;

Joanne, who not only looked after the "chicklets" while we were playing author but also sent us to "to work" each morning with a gourmet picnic lunch;

Andra, Leah, Barrett and Graham, who cheerfully put up with the disruption of their lives so Mommy and Daddy could finish the book;

Ardell, who has an impeccable memory and has always given me her love and support.

But most of all, I want to thank Marilyn Moyer, my sister-in-law. When Steve Simmons left for Toronto, she took two months out of her hectic schedule and, with encouragement, good humour and unending patience, was invaluable in helping bring this book to where we wanted it, to the way you read it today.

Lanny McDonald

I wish to thank the following: Russ Parker, of Calgary Copier, for his support and generosity; Jo Brault, of Calgary Copier, for her computer expertise and patience; Mike Barnett, of CorpSport International, who put the project together; J. Barrie Marshall for his legal advice; Eric Duhatschek and Al Maki, of the *Calgary Herald*, for their opinions; Dave Shoalts, of the *Globe and Mail*, for his help; Wayne Parrish, of the *Toronto Sun*, for his patience; Don Cherry and John Davidson for their memories; and my wife, Sheila, who spent too much of her first pregnancy with her husband being more concerned about a computer terminal than about her.

Steve Simmons

FOREWORD

I was hanging around the Stampede Corral, waiting for the Calgary Flames to finish practising on November 28, 1981, when I decided to go for a walk around the arena. Wandering towards the Flames office, I was surprised to see Bill MacMillan, the general manager of the Colorado Rockies, huddled over a pay telephone in one of the darkened corridors of the building.

"What's up?" I asked MacMillan, wondering why he was still in Calgary, considering that his club, after losing to the Flames the previous night, had already left for Winnipeg.

"Stick around," MacMillan told me. "This should get interesting." He removed his hand from the telephone receiver and resumed talking.

Something was up, but I wasn't sure what. The Flames and the Rockies were rumoured to be talking trade, and the name that was mentioned more often than any other was that of Rob Ramage, the fine young Colorado defenceman. Twice during the Flames' practice that day the session had been stopped. First Don Lever, the club's top left winger, was called from the ice; then Bob MacMillan, Bill's younger brother, was summoned. The remaining players on the ice had an uneasy look about them.

I went to use the pay phone to call my bosses at the *Calgary Sun*, just to let them know something was up. Afterwards I saw Bill MacMillan again, and he gave me the news. MacMillan had just acquired his brother, Bob, and Don Lever in a trade for Lanny McDonald.

Lanny McDonald, I thought. I grew up watching Lanny McDonald. I used to sit in Section 53, Row D, at Maple Leaf Gardens and boo him. Later, after he stopped falling down and started scoring, I cheered for him. But now I was in a different position, as hockey writer for the *Sun*. I was suddenly covering a player I'd been watching since I was sixteen years old—and it felt strange.

After talking to Lever and MacMillan and getting the appropriate responses from the appropriate people, I rushed back to the office to work on the Lanny McDonald story. Alberta's favourite son was coming home, which was front page news. The problem was, McDonald had already flown to Winnipeg with the Rockies and now had to fly back to join the Flames. After several unanswered long distance calls, I finally had him paged at the Winnipeg International Airport. Over the phone, I interviewed McDonald for the first time.

If first impressions mean anything, we didn't seem to hit it off. And my first impression appeared to be accurate, for a while. There was something about McDonald I didn't like, and I sensed that he didn't like something about me. Being a born cynic, in time I discovered what it was I didn't like about McDonald. He was too perfect. He seemed to say all the right things at all the right times. It was as if he had been programmed, cloned by some agent or marketing man. I'd seen his type of professional athlete before, I thought. They smile as they sign children's autographs, then walk away sneering about the damn kids. Another phoney, I thought.

That impression lasted for only a short while. In time, I realized how different Lanny McDonald was. He was the one who would help a handicapped passenger to a seat on the airplane. The one who said the right thing at the right time— and meant it. The one who would pose for pictures with children— and enjoy it. He was different, the consummate professional, if such a thing existed, devoid of scars or closet skeletons. I wasn't the only one who watched in wonderment as McDonald conducted himself with regal deportment: his teammates were also amazed. One by one, the Flames players watched and wondered about McDonald. They, too, came to realize what so many already knew: that McDonald is honest and dedicated and genuine and caring.

I assume his impression of me changed too but I've never really asked him about it. The often strained relationship between reporter and athlete creates an invisible wall, both sides of which are well guarded. But I decided to drop my guard, somewhat. Midway through the 1985–86 season, I asked McDonald if he had ever considered writing a book about his career. He said he had, but never seriously. I asked him if he would seriously consider it, and that was the extent of our conversation. The season went on, and the Flames wound up playing for the Stanley Cup. In all the playoff hoopla, I stopped thinking about our discussion.

Then one summer day, Mike Barnett, of CorpSport International, Lanny's marketing representative, called to ask if I would be interested in writing this book. I told him I would be honoured. As I finish this project, I still feel that way.

A lot of athletes have a lot to tell, but there is only one Lanny King McDonald. This is his story.

Steve Simmons
June, 1987

1

PUNCHED OUT:
THE
IMLACH ERA

Punch Imlach stuck out his right hand and wished me good luck. I refused to accept either the handshake or his good wishes. My only regret on December 28, 1979, was that I didn't hit the general manager of the Maple Leafs when I had the chance.

The day had begun in a particularly aggravating fashion, and it didn't end any better. Because we were in the middle of a losing streak, Punch had called two practices that day. It was one of his ways of punishing players. Two-a-days were unheard of in the middle of the season, except to Punch. Another of his "punishments" was to schedule the first practice so you'd have to drive to the Gardens during rush-hour traffic in the morning and drive home in the afternoon rush hour after the second practice. These were little things, but enough to get to your nerves.

After the second practice, Danny Lemelin, the Leafs trainer, told me to report to the coach's office. Right away I knew something was up. We had lost four or five games in a row, and the rumours were flying. I walked into the office and found, not Floyd Smith, our faltering coach, but Punch. I glared at Imlach. I knew I was gone.

"This is the part of the game that hurts me the worst," Punch began, and in my mind I'm thinking, "You lying son of a bitch."

"Where am I going?" I asked.

"We've traded you to Colorado," Punch answered.

"Who am I going for?"

"Joel Quenneville is going in the same trade with you."

"Well, who am I going for?"

"It's none of your business. It'll be announced later in the day."

End of conversation. I left the coach's office. I was numb. I wanted to do something, but I didn't know what. All I kept thinking was, "Imlach, you absolute ass. You've destroyed my life." By the time I got back to the dressing room, my mind was in total chaos. I couldn't believe what had just happened. My dream had been shattered. No one grows up wanting to play for the Colorado Rockies.

That day, my wife, Ardell, was meeting me after practice so we could go to sign the papers on the house we had just sold. Three weeks earlier, we had moved from our first home to our second. If the trade had happened one day earlier, we would have had two houses to sell instead of just one. The walk to the car was one of the longest of my life— longer than the walk to the coach's office. Ardell was two weeks away from giving birth to our second child. And we had been traded. The whole situation seemed devastating.

I got into the car and looked at Ardell. What do you say to your wife when you think your life has been ruined? I asked Ardell to drive a couple of blocks, just to get away from the Gardens. Then I blurted it out: "We've been traded." It didn't seem important to say where— the big thing was that we were leaving Toronto and the Leafs. I was still in a state of shock, and I couldn't believe that they had done this to us. I was feeling sorry for myself, and for Ardell, both sorry and angry.

I knew I was going to Colorado, but I still didn't know for whom. It wasn't until I spoke with Alan Eagleson's office that I found out the details of the trade. As it turned out, Eagleson not only represented me, but he represented Wilf Paiement, the principal player on the other side of the deal. The trade officially was Joel Quenneville and myself for Paiement and Pat Hickey. While Ardell was two weeks away from giving birth, I found out that Wilf and Susan Paiement were only days away from having their first child. To me, that put everything into perspective about the game. Time, place or circumstances don't matter; when they decide to trade you, they trade you. That's the way the game is played.

To this day, I still believe I was traded out of spite. I think Punch really wanted to show who was boss. It didn't matter how much he hurt the hockey club or tore it apart, he only wanted to make sure everyone knew who was running the team. I used to think it was just a trade, like any other trade until I really thought about it. The more I reflected upon what had happened, the more I realized it was a vindictive deal. Imlach and Sittler were having problems. Let me correct that: Imlach and everyone were having problems. He saw Darryl and his captaincy as a threat and wanted to trade him, but because of the no-trade clause in Sitt's contract, Punch couldn't deal. Imlach had no way to get back at Darryl, so he did the next best thing: He traded Darryl's best friend instead. That happened to be me.

It wasn't Darryl's fault. It was his good fortune to have a no-trade contract, but in the long run, it may have been the worst thing for him. Because of that clause, he spent his last two years in Toronto not enjoying hockey the way he deserved to. Darryl was going through a hell all his own, and it was a shame it had come to that. Maybe for me it was a blessing to get out when I did, but I didn't really think about it that way at the time.

The problems began for Darryl and myself, and for the entire Maple Leafs team, on June 8, 1979, the day Punch Imlach was named the club's general manager. Once Punch replaced Jim Gregory, changes began at Maple Leaf Gardens. Odd changes. Punch started introducing a lot of new rules, and it seemed he was bent on proving who was boss. He had said in the newspapers that we were a bunch of pampered athletes who had been getting our own way for too long.

The problems began before the season did. Darryl Sittler and Mike Palmateer were asked to participate in "Showdown," the between-periods skills segment featured on "Hockey Night in Canada." Imlach said no. A court injunction said yes, and Sittler and Palmateer took part.

There was some Players' Association business to attend to during Punch's first training camp, and I was in the unhappy position of having to deal with him. Heading into that season, the per diem for road trips had been increased by the association, but the Leafs players didn't receive the increase. As player rep, I went to Punch to make sure he knew about the new regulations. He looked at me and said: "I'm running the show here. And this is the way it's going to be." He knew the rules. He was just giving me a hard time about them. Doing my job, I had to have the association send a telex to make sure he complied with the new regulations. For some strange reasons, he turned even the simplest matter into a confrontation.

Those were not the only early problems. Imlach, who wasn't supposed to be the coach but ran the team nonetheless, decided at training camp that there would be no regular roommates on road trips. In most cases, we never knew who we were rooming with until we checked in at a particular hotel. Punch felt that if you roomed with the same person all the time, cliques would form and eventually tear up the team. But I've always been under the impression that if you get along well with someone on the road, you're the better for it. It's hard enough being away from your wife and family; the last thing you want to do is to wind up with a roommate you have trouble living with, someone whose habits are totally different from your own. More than anything else, Punch's idea caused discomfort and discontent. They say that it's the little things that count, and with Punch, it was all the little things— every day— that added up to make everyone unhappy.

When the 1979–80 season began, I found myself right in the middle of a battle I really wanted no part of. Early that season, Punch had forbidden the Leafs players to give television interviews between periods. Darryl was supposed to give an interview in Winnipeg and wasn't allowed to. This started the controversy. Later, as an executive of the Players' Association, he was to have gone to a meeting with the board of governors in New York to discuss the ban on interviews. Punch forbad him to go. The real beef on the team seemed to be between Darryl, as captain, and Punch, but somehow I kept getting involved.

As player rep, I represented the Leafs at that meeting in New York. On the one hand, you're thinking of the players whose interests you are protecting. On the other hand, it's the owners who pay your salary and keep you employed. I found myself in a no-win situation. Leaf owner Harold Ballard vehemently denied that any ban on television interviews was in place. I disagreed: All the players were aware of the situation. I was telling the truth, and I didn't think I was doing anything wrong in standing up to Harold. My first loyalty had to be to the teammates who had elected me to represent them. Harold was furious that I would question him in front of others, and although I never heard about it from him, it got back to me through other channels. This incident may not have been the reason the Leafs traded me, but was one card in a full deck.

If there seemed to be a problem with the Leafs off the ice, on the ice wasn't that much different. Floyd Smith had taken over from Roger Neilson as coach, and it didn't take us long to realize that Floyd was not his own man: He was just a "yes man" carrying out somebody else's orders. That became evident during practices when Punch would come down and talk to Floyd along the boards. Suddenly, our lines would be changed, or we'd be doing a completely different drill. We knew Punch was running the show, and it was difficult to respect Floyd because of this. A lot of us didn't have much confidence in his coaching abilities either, especially after we had played for Roger Neilson.

The sad part was, Floyd was a nice person. But he was a nice person following orders from someone few of us respected. With Floyd, it was as if he were there, but wasn't really there. He'd open his mouth and Punch's words would come out. Discussing anything with Floyd was futile. You knew that your suggestions weren't going to get you anywhere. After a while, it didn't really matter much. We knew the club was in trouble, and we developed a wait-and-see attitude, wondering what was going to happen and who would be the first to go. That's not the attitude or atmosphere that makes for a winning hockey club. Punch Imlach, with his "sixties'-

hockey-hasn't-changed" approach, was running the Leafs— for better or for worse. Mostly for worse.

Imlach's rules continued to grate on everyone. His curfews, both before and after games, were earlier than any others in hockey: 10:30 the night before the game. Hell, you couldn't even catch the late movie at the Plaza! After a game, you hardly had time for a "beer and a bite." Punch decreed that players weren't allowed in the offices at Maple Leaf Gardens unless they were wearing jackets and ties. Maybe you needed a question answered, or you might be called to the office for something, and unless you had the required clothing, you couldn't go. And after all, how many times does a player wear a jacket and tie to practice? Punch seemed to come up with meaningless rules that only made things more difficult for the guys and did absolutely nothing for the betterment of the team. The list of grievances were growing.

By then we were playing just to survive. Even if it has the talent, especially if it's not being led in the right direction, you can take the most talented team in the world, but with brutal direction, it'll end up going nowhere. That's where we were going. We were going nowhere fast.

The season progressed and little changed. The team wasn't accomplishing much. Roger had given Darryl, as captain, a fair amount of responsibility, and Punch seemed more intent on stripping that power from Darryl than he was on anything else. Floyd continued coaching, with little success. As the season grew longer and feelings grew harder, it became obvious that something would have to be done. No one knew just what that something would be.

Then we went to Buffalo one day to play the Sabres, and we knew something was up. There were four or five extra equipment bags, and the feeling then was that the Leafs had made a trade with the Sabres. We thought that players would be exchanged before the game, but it never happened.

Earlier that afternoon, Pat Boutette had been traded to Hartford for a player named Bob Stephenson— someone that nobody knew much about. It was a trade, but it wasn't the trade everyone had been expecting. We knew Punch was working on something— we figured it was big— but we had lost in Buffalo that night, and there was no trade. When we got back to Toronto, we all gathered at Paddy's house. Some players were offering him condolences, some were congratulating him for getting a parole from our situation. (Paddy went on to have several productive years in Hartford and later in Pittsburgh. Stephenson played 14 games for the Maple Leafs.)

Of all the rumours that were going around at this time, none of them involved me. I guess that's the best way to be traded, with no anxiety prior to the deal. It just happens. Unexpectedly. There's enough difficulty involved in being traded that you don't need any added aggravations.

Ten years ago I would have been shocked if someone had told me that I would wind up with three teams. I started as a Maple Leaf, and I expected to end that way. Then the news came and I thought my life was over. A part of me died the day the Maple Leafs traded me. Today a part of me feels that the trade may have been one of the best things that ever happened to me. But at the time, I sure didn't feel like that.

The day of the trade was the longest day of my life but it probably went the fastest. Ardell's family was with us in Toronto for the Christmas season, and as soon as we walked in the door they knew something was wrong. Everybody's first thought was that something had happened to the baby. "No," I said, "we've been traded." Lucille, Ardell's mom, putting her arms around us both and trying to put things into perspective, said, "As long as the baby's fine, we can deal with anything."

Our support team grew, and the phone didn't stop ringing. Not only were friends calling, but the media, looking for the "real" story, had a job to do. In retrospect, one of the truest comments came from Andra Kelly, who called Ardell to assure her that, in the months ahead, we'd look back on this day and it wouldn't seem as painful. "Besides," she said, "Colorado is a paradise." As hard as it was to believe her then, it turned out Andra was right.

Another call we remember and can laugh about now came from Graeme Clark, our good friend and accountant. "I can't believe you got traded," he consoled. "But think of it this way: Look at the tax breaks you'll have in the States."

I replied, "That's the last thing on my mind right now, Graeme."

"Maybe now, Lanny, but wait until April. You'll feel better then!"

The trade was big news in Toronto, big enough to get the banner headline in the paper. Big enough to beat out President Jimmy Carter's condemnation of the Soviet invasion of Afghanistan— at least, that's what *The Toronto Star* thought!

As with the trading of Boutette, the team rallied round, and our home became the meeting place for our friends the day before I left for Denver. That December night, a group of players came over to say their goodbyes and wish us well. Darryl and Wendy were the last to leave. The four of us stood there looking at each other, wanting to say so much but not able to find the words. We knew things would never be the same.

Looking back, it almost seemed as if Punch wanted to trade me to the worst possible team— the Rockies, one of the worst franchises in league history. The timing of the trade only created more of a problem. A player never looks at the positive side of a trade. You always think that your team has given up on you. It's difficult to look at it from the other side— another team wants you. You always think the worst, and it takes a while to get your head settled and to figure everything out.

While I was on my way to Denver, the new Leafs— with Wilf Paiement and Pat Hickey— were playing their first home game. I wasn't there and can only go by what I was told, but I felt vindicated: Apparently, I wasn't the only one who felt betrayed. Outside Maple Leaf Gardens, fans protested the deal. They marched in front of the Gardens carrying signs and banners and making a lot of noise. The same fans who booed me in my first two years were now protesting the trade, carrying signs that read, "Bad Punch Spoils a Party," and chanting, "Nobody can do it like McDonald can," from the old McDonald's commercial.

I was really touched by the fans' support, and it somehow softened the devastation both Ardell and I were feeling. Just knowing that people were behind us was a comfort, and I still have a soft spot in my heart for those Toronto fans. I had turned their thinking around about me. And that hadn't been easy.

Meanwhile, inside the Gardens, my dear friend Darryl, born to be captain of the Maple Leafs, had taken the "C" from his sweater. Not as a protest against my trade, but in frustration with the whole situation. I may have been gone from the scene, but Punch continued to damage the spirit of the Leafs, and sadly, Darryl had to be a large part of it.

It's hard to recall what I said at the time, but in the *Rocky Mountain News*, a Denver paper, I was quoted about what was happening in Toronto.

Don't feel sorry for me. I'm one of the fortunate ones, getting a second chance somewhere. Feel sorry for the guys staying behind on a disappointed, disorganized, disgruntled hockey team. That situation in Toronto boiled down to Punch Imlach against the world. He has a vendetta against everyone.

I really thought at times Punch was happy to see us lose. Jim Gregory built the team, and now Punch is trying to tear that team down. Times have changed, and I think the game has passed Punch by.

The way he's treating Sittler is very sad. Darryl is a credit to hockey; he doesn't deserve that type of abuse. I think he'll be the next to go. They're after him, and have been since Day One. It's really a shame, because they (the players) are a class bunch of guys.

It isn't Coach [Floyd] Smith, it's Coach Imlach. Smitty is just his "yes man." That's all he is.

If the players stick together, they can make it. I'm glad I stuck up for what is right.

I don't feel any differently now.

2

GOOD DREAMS AND NIGHTMARES

Dreams really do come true, I thought to myself as I sat in the stands of Maple Leaf Gardens on that September day in 1973 when I first reported to the Toronto Maple Leafs. The building was dark, and I wanted to be alone, just to have time to think. It was an unbelievable feeling sitting there. I'd finally made it. There I was at the Gardens, about to begin playing for the Maple Leafs, the team I had cheered for like crazy as a kid. I sat there, realizing that everything I had dreamed about had come true.

I was Lanny McDonald, twenty-year-old farm boy from Craigmyle, Alberta, population 103. First draft choice, fourth overall. Professional hockey player. Toronto Maple Leaf. Boy, did that sound good!

I was brought back to earth quickly when I checked into the Westbury Hotel, where the players were based for training camp. The front desk told me I had a "roomie," Ian Turnbull, who had also been drafted in the first round by the Leafs. I still remember strutting into the room in my three-piece, black-and-white checked suit, complete with black velvet bow tie (I was sure it was in fashion... somewhere). Lounging on the bed, in levis and T-shirt, and strumming a guitar was my new roommate from Montreal. He looked up, quit playing and said, "Is that suit for real?" The bubble had burst.

On the first day of camp nothing could go wrong, or so I thought. I'll never forget the anxiety I felt as I got ready for those first workouts of training camp. When you go on the ice, you want to touch the puck, and yet, you don't want to touch it. You want to get the puck and have it forever, as if you were playing with the kids on your block. And you don't want to get near it, in case you screw up. Despite my trepidation, I was still confident. Unfortunately, my confidence didn't last much longer than that first day.

It was during one of the early exhibition games that I began to wonder what I had got myself into. We were playing the Red Wings in Kalamazoo and I probably got hit about 15 times in that game and knocked down 12. You keep track of those kinds of statistics when you're a rookie. With bruising come questions. Serious questions. Am I not good enough? Am I not fast enough? Are things happening so fast here that I'm not realizing what's going on? I was shaken for a while. Your mind starts playing tricks on you. It didn't take long for the wide-eyed optimism of that first camp day to turn to near panic. Everything seemed to be going wrong. For the first time ever, I was questioning whether I could play. And I was scared of the answer.

I had a new centreman and a new roommate on the

road, an old hero of mine—Davey Keon. Starting out with the Maple Leafs was one thing. Starting out with Davey Keon was another. I quickly found that the Keon I had watched on television for so many years wasn't the guy I had built him up to be. To understand the problems I had with Keon, you have to understand the times.

The World Hockey Association was in its second year of existence, and the salary structure of hockey had gone totally out of whack, with the two leagues vying for players' services. The Leafs had some veterans like Keon and Norm Ullman—truly great players who had dedicated a lot of years to hockey—and suddenly, a bunch of us young guys were making pretty good money, even though we hadn't proved anything. All because of the tug-of-war between the WHA and NHL.

There certainly was some resentment from a guy like Keon. Let's face it, he'd been around a long time; but still, I was disappointed: He was the player I idolized as a kid. Now, as one of those "veteran players," I can understand what he was feeling.

We didn't click, on the ice or off. I was put on his right wing, and right from the start, it didn't work out. We didn't play the same styles. He was a skilled skater and playmaker; I was just trying to make an impression. He was ready. I was struggling.

The thing I'll never forget about Keon was his aloofness. I realize now that's just the way he was. And in Davey's defence, he was going through a difficult time away from the game and had a lot more to deal with than most of us were aware of. Fortunately, things turned out for him, and now when I see Davey, we get along pretty well. I think both sides understand each other today more than we did then.

By the time the season began, I was in the starting lineup, even though I'm not sure I deserved to be. I was still playing alongside Keon but no longer rooming with him. After Keon, I wound up with a new roommate, Inge Hammarstrom, and we hit it off right away. At least the off-ice problems seemed over.

I was excited about the start of the regular season. I was making my debut against Buffalo, cruising along in my first NHL game with two assists. Not a bad way to debut. It was as if all the problems of training camp had magically disappeared once the puck dropped to begin the regular season. I felt like I was turning the corner; I felt like I belonged. Then, without warning, it happened.

I played one pro game without a helmet. I won't play another. The Sabres were on a two-man power play on opening night, and I was in the penalty box. Leaving the box, I rushed back into the play, and one of the first things I ran into was Richard Martin of the Sabres. Maybe it was the other way around—maybe Martin ran into me. I saw him coming at me with a hip check, and I jumped, thinking I could get out of the way of the check. But I caught my skates on his pants and was propelled into a somersault. The judges would have scored it about a nine. I came down and landed on my head. The rest I don't remember all that well. I got the usual "What's your name?" "Where are you?" treatment and wound up with six stitches over my eye, about eight more in the back of my head and one whopper of a concussion. It was a definite lesson. That was the only game I played without a helmet. After leaving junior hockey, where helmets were mandatory, I thought I'd take the big-league approach and go without a helmet. I quickly found out I was just being stupid.

Martin's hit proved to be more of a setback that I ever would have believed it could be. After opening the season against the Sabres, the Leafs travelled to Philadelphia for the second game. I spent the night in Wellesley Hospital and flew to Philadelphia on the day of the game, expecting to play. But I didn't. All I can remember of that night is sleeping in the dressing room.

I just couldn't keep my eyes open. I slept through most of the game, and I slept on the flight home as well. In fact, some critics might insist that after running into Rick Martin, I slept through most of my rookie season!

The two assists I had in Game 1 were one of the few highlights of a very long and unproductive rookie season. But I did manage to score my first NHL goal—a game winner at the Montreal Forum—set up by Davey Keon. But I didn't get many more. It wasn't the type of season I had dreamed about, and it didn't take me long to realize that dreams and professional hockey don't necessarily coincide. The season seemed longer than 76 games, mainly because I didn't play the way I wanted to. A lot of people were saying I was a flop, and I was putting more pressure on myself because the other rookies were playing so well.

Borje Salming was doing what he was expected to do, but the real surprise of the group was Ian Turnbull. Ian was the third pick of the three first-round choices the Leafs had, and the club wasn't really sure what to expect from him. I think they knew Borje could play; they hoped Inge could play. No one realized just how much talent Turnbull really had. Ian played as well as Borje did, and he certainly played a lot more and a lot better than Bob Neely or myself. In time, because we were single, because we were rookies and because Inge and I roomed together, Ian, Inge and I became good friends.

Perhaps the nicest thing about hockey is the friends you make. If anyone had told me that I could have been friends with Ian Turnbull, I think I would have laughed, and I'm sure he would have too. If I called something white, he'd call it black. We were total opposites: He was city; I was country. He grew up in Montreal and had what I considered to be "big city" ideas. His entire approach to life was different from mine. Yet we got along well. No one could have disliked Inge. He was a very special, down-to-earth person. He only wanted to do his job and play the best he could. His sincerity and honesty were unparalleled. The only real problem was, Inge and I weren't playing all that well, and I think that brought us closer together. Maybe misery loves company.

If there was an unsung leader of the Leafs at the time, that man was Ronnie Ellis. He didn't say much, but he let his actions on the ice speak for themselves. I tried to pick up all the good things he did. Not realizing he was as good as he was, he was never satisfied with himself. He tried to run right through guys. His legs were always moving, and I learned a tremendous amount just by watching him. It wasn't that I was doing so much wrong; it was just that I didn't have the confidence to do anything right. I couldn't get the confidence to go from my head to my hands, to my feet, and so I couldn't perform the way I knew I was capable of performing. It was as if I had a mental block.

Like Keon, Ellis was a hero of mine when I was growing up. I still looked upon Ellis that way when I played for the Maple Leafs. There are times in life when you expect too much from people, but Ellis was the type who gave and never stopped giving. I wanted to be just like him, and I still think of Ronnie as a hero.

My stint on Keon's line didn't last long. Early in the season, I was dispatched to a line called The Black Aces, with centre George Ferguson and left winger Errol Thompson. We were the fourth line, the type of line who didn't play much at home. But when we went to Philadelphia to face the rough, tough Flyers, we were on the ice an awful lot. At that time, the Leafs weren't known as a physical team, but our line didn't care— we just wanted to play. I guess that was part of the growing-up process in the league.

I kept thinking things would get better, but they didn't that first season. Let's face it, the expectations were high, especially considering how well other rookies were playing: Tom Lysiak in Atlanta, John Davidson in St. Louis and Andre Savard in Boston. And Denis Potvin was a standout for the Islanders. Bob Gainey was proving himself in Montreal. Not me, though, and I was putting extra pressure on myself by looking at their statistics and feeling I should be competitive with them.

Some people went out of their way to try and make it easier for me, though. It seemed every time I was really down, I wound up talking with Jim Gregory, the general manager of the Leafs. I always felt Jim was the kind of guy you could really talk to. He was always there to listen if I had something on my mind. If he thought I should do things differently, he told me. He once said to me, "Look Lanny, don't put pressure on yourself to make it happen today or tomorrow. We signed this agreement for five years, and we'll reevaluate it after five years, not after six months." Those talks always gave me a lot of confidence, just knowing he wasn't giving up on me when others were.

Eddie Johnston, one of the veteran goaltenders, really went out of his way to help me feel at home. E.J. was probably thirty-four at the time, and I really thought of him as "old." Why does thirty-four seem so young now? I learned one very important lesson from Eddie that I've never forgotten. I vowed then that when I became a veteran on a hockey club, I'd remember what it was like to be a rookie; I'd remember what it felt like when a vet made a simple gesture of friendship, and how much that single action could make a first-year player feel as if he belonged. Since then, my attitude has always been, hey, let's help each other, we're all in this business together.

If there was a highlight of that first season, other than the first goal, it came the day before I ended my season. I scored my first career hattrick against the New York Rangers and could not believe how excited, happy and relieved I was; I felt that I was finally turning it around.

My exhilaration, however, was brief. In practice the next day, I got hit by Willy Brossart and separated my shoulder. That kind of summed up the way the whole first year went. Every time something good happened, something bad followed it. The regular season ended, and that hot-shot first-round pick— me— had scored 14 goals and 16 assists, numbers that didn't exactly justify my existence.

That season we went to Boston to start the playoffs, and by then I was almost healthy enough to return to the lineup. Then my fiancée, Ardell, called from Medicine Hat. Her sixteen-year-old brother, Gerard, had died after an asthma attack that day. I didn't know what to do— I was numb. I couldn't believe that anything like this could happen to someone so full of life, so anxious to grow up, so close to being a man. In the past couple of years, Gerard and I had become good friends, almost as close as brothers. I didn't want to imagine what life without him would be like.

Coach Red Kelly said, "I'll have you on the next plane home, and you come back when you're ready."

I went home. The Leafs lost four straight games to the Boston Bruins. I never did make it back that season.

3

YOUNG
AND
INNOCENT

I was first introduced to Richard Sorkin in my final year of junior hockey at Medicine Hat. Picking an agent then was very different from picking an agent today. In truth, junior players had little say in choosing who would represent them in those days. It was a "slave trade" of sorts, with the junior clubs making deals with certain agents and all but assuring them that they would represent the club's top players as they turned professional.

It was something like the old sponsorship setup. If you played for the Toronto Marlboros, you were Maple Leaf property. Well, in the early 1970s, if you played for the Medicine Hat Tigers, you wound up with Richard

Sorkin as your agent. That's the way it worked: The agent got his player, the player got his agent.

That year, four of us playing for Medicine Hat were considered pretty good prospects. Tom Lysiak, of course, was the most highly regarded of the four—and he was the first of us to be drafted. I was second, Bob Gassoff was third and Jimmy McCrimmon was fourth. All four of us signed with Sorkin, but I was the last to do so.

The first time I met Sorkin I knew there was something about him that I didn't like. You know how it sometimes is: you meet someone new and instantly take a liking to him. Well, it just wasn't that way with Sorkin. It wasn't that I *disliked* him; he just wasn't my kind of guy. A kid from the West would label him a "typical" New Yorker. He talked a lot, was cocky and very brash. He seemed particularly overbearing to someone who hadn't been exposed to the world beyond the Western Canada Hockey League.

Even though I wasn't sure about Sorkin, he still became my agent. It wasn't long before I realized that I had to put more faith in my own instincts. I made a mistake signing with Sorkin: At the time, however, I just didn't know how much of a mistake.

Everything was going so smoothly—the negotiations with the Leafs, my dealings with Sorkin. Everything. Until the press conference to announce my signing with the Leafs. After coming to terms with the Leafs, Sorkin and I agreed on one thing: Details of my contract would remain private. And they did. Until the press conference. The late Red Burnett, who covered hockey for *The Toronto Star*, described the press conference in the *Star* of June 8, 1973:

> Other than admitting McDonald had received a fine multi-year contract, Gregory refused to reveal details. McDonald's agent, Dick Sorkin, a former sports writer, had no such reluctance.

"Lanny received the best contract ever given a junior grad," he offered.

How did it compare with the deal the New York Islanders gave Denis Potvin, the first junior grad drafted into the NHL?

"It is a much better deal," he answered. "I hear Potvin got $500,000 for four years. The Leafs topped that. With the built-in investments and deferred payment clauses, he could become the best paid man in the league."

When I read those comments, I almost swallowed my tongue. That's how upset I was. Through no fault of my own, the pressure had begun. The headlines told the story: "Lanny in High Income Bracket"; "McDonald Hits Jackpot"; "Lanny Richest Graduate"; "Record Contract for Junior." It doesn't seem that bad now, considering how things worked out in the end, but to a twenty-year-old, just coming out of junior, it sure wasn't the way I would have chosen to burst on to the Maple Leaf scene.

Obviously, the competition between the NHL and the WHA was fierce then; the Cleveland Crusaders, who had drafted me, wanted me as much as the Maple Leafs did. But I wanted the Maple Leafs. And, as proud as I was about the contract I had signed, the last thing I wanted to do was let it be known how much I had signed for. Don't get me wrong. I wasn't ashamed. But I did believe that salary is a private matter. I wanted my play to do the talking for me. All that Sorkin's comments did was to put extra pressure on me and cause further animosity towards me among the older players on the Leafs.

After the initial contract negotiations, I got on with the business of hockey, and Sorkin got on with the business of handling my finances. Still, I wasn't happy about him, despite the deal he got for me.

The contract I signed with the Leafs was for five seasons, and while the first season had barely begun, there were financial matters to attend to that required professional attention—more than I was capable of giving myself or of getting from Sorkin. I had just decided to join the Eagleson group when the story on Sorkin broke in the papers.

Richard Sorkin had squandered more than $1 million belonging to some 50 clients, almost all of whom were NHL players. One was my old linemate, Tommy Lysiak. In 1977, Richard Sorkin was sentenced to prison, and I kept thinking how lucky I was that I got away when I did. Some guys weren't so lucky. They lost their life savings.

But I didn't escape unscathed. Just after the story broke, the tax people came knocking on the door and said I owed them almost $40,000 in back taxes. "That can't be true," I said. "I always paid my taxes." I had copies of the cheques to prove it. It had to be a mistake.

It wasn't. It was Sorkin. I was another of his victims.

He had written out cheques to the government on my behalf, photocopied them for my records but never sent them in. Suddenly, the government was banging on my door, telling me I had 48 hours to come up with $38,000.

First of all, I didn't have $38,000. Secondly, Ardell and I were expecting our first child. And, to top it all off, we had just purchased our first home. The timing couldn't have been worse, if there is such a thing as "good" timing in a matter like this. We were scared. Where were we going to come up with that kind of money? In that short a time?

After coming to grips with what had happened, my first instinct was to go to my new agent, Alan Eagleson, and ask him what to do. His advice was to go to Jim Gregory, explain the whole situation and see what could be done. I didn't feel comfortable about that, but it turned out that Eagleson was right. Gregory handled the situation the same way he handled just about everything else: smoothly, professionally, quickly. Gregory wrote a cheque for $38,000, and all he said to me was, "Pay the money back when you can."

By the end of the season, the money had been returned. My problems with Sorkin were over, and I felt fortunate to have people like Eagleson and Gregory on my side.

4

FROM RED
TO
ROGER

I've often wondered what would have happened to me
had I not come across a man named Red Kelly. I've also
wondered how he could be so patient for so long. On a
team like the Maple Leafs, in a town like Toronto, where
pressure gets put on a club by all kinds of outside for-
ces, Coach Red Kelly stuck by me when just about
everyone else had written me off. Maybe he saw something that others didn't. For me to struggle as long as I
did and not go to the minors was incredible. I don't
think I've ever sat down and asked Red why he hung in
there with me. It was always one of those unanswered
questions. One thing is certain, though: I'm eternally
grateful to him, because I'm not sure I could have made
it without him.

Despite Red's confidence in me, my second season started no differently than the first. Except for one factor: I had been moved from right wing to left wing. For my entire hockey life, which at the time constituted 16 years, I had considered myself a natural right winger. I shot right. I knew the position. It was natural. Suddenly, I found myself on the left side, plunged into an experiment that lasted all of one regular season game. The thinking then was, if I didn't work out on right wing the year before, maybe I'd work out on the other side. Red may have been sticking by me, but he was also trying anything he could to get me going.

My goal total increased from 14 to 17 in my second year, not exactly the quantum leap that would justify the high draft pick the Leafs had used to choose me, never mind their financial investment. But the statistics don't really tell the whole story, and my second year was a lot better than my first. At least, that's what I kept telling myself. There were actually times when I did play well. But there were also many times when I played in the same frustrating style that got me in trouble during my rookie season. The question of whether I'd ever make it remained in my mind, and not just in my mind: It was in management's and in the fans' minds as well.

I'm not sure if the problem was with my skating, or if the pace was that much quicker or if my confidence was shot to the point where I couldn't handle the puck and keep my head up at the same time. I just don't know. It seemed like I had my head down the whole time, and I just couldn't seem to play any differently. I was like a radar signal for an oncoming defenceman: "Hit McDonald, because his head is always down." It was a case of "Here comes the kid; it should be easy pickings tonight." Frankly, I was lucky I survived it all. The second season was barely better than the first, and the third started out like nothing at all had changed. After

15 games, I had about two goals, and it was the same old story all over again. I tried to tell myself that it wasn't happening again, but I knew it was.

Oddly enough, the biggest break I got was from a writer, not from a player, and I'll never forget it.

Frank Orr, an institution among hockey writers, wrote an article in *The Toronto Star* saying something like, "Hey, let's get off this kid's back and give him a chance. He has all the potential in the world, let's let it happen." The article came out on the day of a game, and I must have read it about ten times. I couldn't sleep that afternoon. I got back up and read it a few more times, then headed for the game. That was one of the turning points. I really believe that. It was if people were looking at me differently. It gave me a renewed confidence. Someone out there, other than my wife, was telling me I could make it. That was all I needed, and I went from there. That night I didn't do anything special, but I felt the turnaround was coming soon.

What made me appreciate Frank Orr's article so much was the fact that he went against what most people were saying at the time. In fact, for some reason, Don Ramsay (a hockey writer at the *Globe and Mail*) seemed to want my head on a platter; he spent a lot of time trying to convince people that I'd never make it. I couldn't understand why he was doing it, and I really was hurt. Coming from the West, maybe my ideas were a little different, but I figured that if you were giving it your best shot, and things weren't working out, a bit of patience could do a lot. On the one hand, two years is probably a long time to expect someone to be patient. But when it's your life some writer is toying with, it's awfully difficult. We had words a few times, and I admit there were a couple of instances when I would have liked to grab Don Ramsay and shake him!

But, it doesn't work out that way. Not in this business.

This man caused me a lot of pain, and I hate to even give him credence in this book, but he taught me an invaluable lesson: Once you're in the public eye, you're subject to public scrutiny.

Everyone told me that feuding with the press was a mistake. So, I tried another approach. I didn't stop talking to Ramsay the way I would have liked to do. I tried to make things easier between us: I made myself as accessible as possible so that I was available for interviews. It didn't work. Nothing did. Ramsay made life miserable for Ardell and me, and, as things turned out, I eventually ended up not talking to him. Years later, he surfaced in Winnipeg as the public relations man for the Jets, and let's just say that it was a mutual understanding that pleasantries were never exchanged. Frankly, I don't know if he ever changed his tune about me. I let my playing speak for me. I figured that was the best way to solve all the problems, and in my third NHL season, suddenly things were beginning to work out.

I got going at just the right time, or so I learned some years later. By the time I'd started my third year in Toronto, there were trade rumours that Atlanta was interested in me. The thinking was, the Flames had Tommy Lysiak, my junior centre, and if I were reunited with him, maybe I could get things back together. Rumour had it that I would go to Atlanta and Curt Bennett would come to the Leafs. To this day Jim Gregory says the talks were never that serious. But Cliff Fletcher, the Flames' general manager, tells a different story. Apparently, the deal had been agreed upon, but it was put off for the weekend. This was all going on about the same time Orr wrote his *Toronto Star* article.

We went on a road trip to St. Louis, and I scored two goals that night. The next night I got another goal, and after that, the trade was off. The St. Louis game was the first of a seven-game road trip, and when it was all over, I had scored five goals and had four assists. Finally, my troubles were behind me. After starting the season with five points in my first 15 games, I ended it with 37 goals and 90 points—more than my first two years combined in both goals and assists. After that season, I averaged 44 goals a season for the next seven campaigns, scoring more in that time period than any other NHL players except Mike Bossy and Marcel Dionne. The good times had begun, and I wanted the puck all the time. Suddenly, defencemen weren't lining me up; I was lining them up. Happy days were here again.

By this time, the Leafs had begun forming the nucleus of a young and exciting club. Keon, Ullman and Paul Henderson had gone to the WHA. Darryl Sittler had developed into the star the Maple Leafs knew he would become. Two former Black Aces, Errol Thompson and myself, each scored more than 40 goals. Borje Salming, Ian Turnbull and Brian Glennie gave us the beginnings of a young, strong defence. And a guy named Tiger Williams had joined the team, ready to take on the world. We were all ready—but not necessarily able. The next two seasons ended in similar fashion. We beat the Pittsburgh Penguins in the opening round of the playoffs and then lost to the Philadelphia Flyers in the quarter finals. The team was ready to make a move in the standings. But under Red Kelly, we had won only 31, 31, 34 and 33 games in four successive seasons. It was time for a change, and everyone—including Red—knew it.

Red Kelly was too good a guy to be a coach. As I look back now, he was too nice and probably not hard enough on the players who needed a boot in the rear once in a while—myself included. I have the utmost respect for Red as a hockey player, and he was understanding and compassionate during the most difficult times of my life. Red's only downfall was that he should have been a lot tougher on all of us. I won't say we took advantage of him, but sometimes we did play too much on his goodwill. Red was well liked as a coach, but it seemed we needed a more structured setup.

I'll never forget the day Jim McKenny brought his son, Jason, to practice. I guess Jason was about five years old at the time. Jimmy and Red came off the ice at the same time. They both walked into the dressing room, and Jason looked up at Red.

"Aren't you Red Kelly?"

"Yes, I am."

"My mom thinks you're a terrible coach," Jason said.

McKenny, the quick wit that he is, interrupted the conversation to say nervously, "But my wife and I don't agree on a lot of things, Red." As a parent, Jimmy must have been thinking that this was one of those times when the old saying, "Kids should be seen and not heard," really fit.

The one thing you didn't expect from Red was swearing. He'd say "hang" instead of "hell," or he'd call a player a "sea cook and bottle washer." I remember one game where we really stunk in the first period. Red stormed into the dressing room immediately following the period, looked us all in the eye and shouted, "Jeez, you guys aren't playing worth hell!"

Well, Jimmy McKenny got right up and said, "Hey, look Red, I know we're playing bad, but you don't have to swear."

With that, Red got so angry he left the room, slamming the door so hard that it jammed. There were about five seconds of silence before the whole dressing room erupted in laughter. We actually turned around and won the darn game, but that was one of the few times Red ever showed that side of him. I can't recall ever hearing him swear again!

Personally, I never really knew what to think of Red as a coach. But Red had his ways; sometimes they worked, and sometimes they didn't. However, there were some things that he did very well. One of those was to create diversions simply to take the pressure off his players. Usually, he came up with theories around playoff time, just when you were really starting to feel the heat.

One year, Red introduced us to "pyramid power." We walked into the dressing room one day, and there were these silver pyramids that were supposed to centre your energies. Naturally, our first reaction was that the long season had finally got to Red—that he'd passed the point of no return. But when I sat back and thought about it, it was a damn good idea. He was taking the pressure off us by going public with one of his crazy schemes. Who knows if it worked or not? But I do know one thing: A lot of the guys may have scoffed at the pyramids publicly, but in the security of the dressing room we were sitting under them, putting our sticks under them and sometimes even plopping our skates under them to see if we could reap some of the supposed magic. I know I was one of the ones giving it a try!

That wasn't the only odd move Red pulled. The next year it was positive ions. We sort of understood the pyramids and the power you were supposed to get from them. Positive ions were something we kidded about a lot. I never did know how they worked, but the funny thing was, you got a good feeling from Red's schemes, the feeling you were going to produce better. But both years we would up being eliminated by the Philadelphia Flyers in the playoffs. In the end, pyramid power and positive ions weren't enough. The Leafs let Red Kelly go as coach, and I, for one, was sad about that.

Red was the only NHL coach I had played for, so I could only compare him with junior hockey coaches. The guy who taught me the most hockey before the NHL was John Chapman, who was my tier-two coach with the Lethbridge Sugar Kings. Chapman wasn't well known then, but he later became prominent when he coached all the Sutter brothers before they made the NHL. Chappy knew how to teach hockey. After playing for him, I went to Medicine Hat, where Jack Shupe was a totally different kind of coach. He expected you to know things before you got there. What I liked about playing for Jack was the way he treated us—like men. He really cared about the players and had great enthusiasm for the game. The point is, I didn't have a lot of background in coaches when I got to Toronto, and I wasn't sure what to expect from Red Kelly. The one thing I did know was that I liked him.

When Red was let go at the end of the 1976–77 season, it was really a mutual parting of the ways. Red was ready to get on with his life. He was disappointed about leaving, but I think he knew that we, as a team, were ready for a change.

My relationship with Red Kelly didn't end when he left the Leafs. We'd become good friends with the Kellys, and our families still keep in touch. Andra Kelly, Red's wife, initiated a skating program for the blind, and Ardell helped her teach these classes. When our eldest daughter was born, we named her after this wonderful, caring lady. We still value our friendship with the Kellys. I think it is a friendship that will always be cherished, and it began as an honest relationship between a player who was struggling and a coach who cared.

When a club changes coaches, no one ever knows what to expect. But in the case of the 1977 Leafs, the uncertainty was even greater. No one had heard much about Roger Neilson, but when Roger took over the Leafs, it was a most exciting time. He was such a totally different personality from Red that he caught everybody off guard. It was exciting to see what he was trying to do with our hockey club. He had put together two scoring lines and a checking line that could stop just about anybody; and he put Mike Palmateer in goal. Mike wasn't just ready to stop the puck, he was ready to save the world. We were beginning to feel we could take it to anybody!

There were times, especially at the start, when we didn't understand Roger's coaching techniques. But it didn't take us long to realize one thing: He was two or three steps ahead of the opposing coaches. Whenever we played Montreal, the games became cat and mouse matches, not only over which team would win but over which coach would win. Scotty Bowman was coaching the Canadiens then, and Roger considered playing them the ultimate test. We had some great games.

Roger was years ahead of himself, doing things that wouldn't be done in hockey for some time. He wasn't afraid of anything new. I remember one game in Pittsburgh: We were losing by three or four goals in the second period when we got a two-man advantage. Roger shocked everybody by pulling the goalie, and we had six skaters against their three. We didn't win, but with Roger, life was never dull!

I'm not sure Roger has ever been given the credit he deserves for being an innovator. He came up with all kinds of new ways of running power plays and penalty killing. He was one of the first coaches I know of who switched wingers on the power play. He took the right-hand shooter, like myself, and had us play the left side on the power play, for the better angle. Now everyone does that. He wasn't afraid of using pick plays. A pick play can be an effective weapon, especially on the power play. As in basketball, one of your players lines up against one of their players, effectively blocking him out of the play. Instead of having a six-on-five power play, suddenly it's a five-on-four, and the offensive players have more room to manoeuvre. At the time, no one did it. Now everyone is doing it. The amazing thing about playing for Roger was that you never knew what he was going to do next.

In his first season, we finished with 92 points, 11 more than the previous season, the most points a Leaf team had garnered since 1950–51, back in the days of the 70-game schedule. The whole city of Toronto was turned on to the Maple Leafs and looking forward to the playoffs. But not half as much as the team itself was.

We had little trouble in the first round, eliminating the Los Angeles Kings in two straight games. (At that time, the opening round was a best-of-three series. It later graduated to a best-of-five, and it is now a best-of-seven. No wonder the season keeps getting longer.) After beating the Kings we were set to play the New York Islanders, who had finished third overall with 111 points in league standings. With Mike Bossy, Denis Potvin and Bryan Trottier, they were considered the best team in the league next to the Canadiens. Still, with Roger behind the bench and Palmateer in goal, we figured we had a better chance than anyone was giving us. Even after losing the first two of the series, the second game in overtime, we figured we had a chance. Even after Borje Salming, our all-star defenceman, went down with an injury, we figured we had a chance. Call it blind faith, call it anything you want. There was a feeling on that Maple Leaf's team, a feeling that something great was about to happen.

After losing the first two games, we won our two games at home, and Palmateer was unbelievable. The Islanders only scored once in the two games. We went back to the Island, confident as heck we were going to win the series, but again, we lost 2–1 in overtime when Bobby Nystrom scored the winner. I, for one, was feeling especially badly. Early in overtime, I thought I had scored the winning goal. My backhand beat Chico Resch but hit the post.

If there was one thing that got on our nerves during the first three games at the Nassau Coliseum, it was the music from the public address system. Every time the

Islanders went on or off the ice, the song "We are the Champions" blared. Not only was the song driving us nuts, but it seemed somewhat presumptuous of them to call themselves champions when they hadn't won anything.

We went home for Game 6 and thrashed New York in one of only two one-sided games in the series. They won the first game easily; we won the sixth. We had been sticking to Roger's game plan, playing physical hockey where conventional thinking said you couldn't play physically. We had already lost Salming, and I injured my wrist early in the series, coming off a Potvin check. I had a broken bone, and before every game I had to get my wrist frozen, then taped. It hurt like hell, but that wasn't my only problem. I was wearing one of those caged helmets to protect a broken nose. Normally these things bother you, but this was the playoffs. And Roger had a way of psyching everyone up. First he would show us a five-minute clip of things we were doing wrong. Then he'd counteract that with a ten-minute film of good defensive plays, hits, goals and incredible saves. It got us pumped, and when the puck was dropped we were ready to play!

Throughout the series there had been two constants. The brilliance of Palmateer and the phenomenal play of Ian Turnbull. When Salming went down, Turnbull took over. He became the quarterback. He wanted the puck, the way Salming always did. Ian was like a man possessed. I don't think he ever played as well, before that series or after it.

Game 7 was much like the rest of the series, with the score tight all the way. The difference in this game was that the Islanders were out-playing us terribly. Killing us is a better way of putting it. I figure they should have beat us three times over. But they didn't. I think that one play in particular sent us a message that it was our night. Trottier was in front of our net with the puck, and Palmateer was out of the goal. Trottier let go with what looked like a sure goal, and Palmateer, sprawling, stuck out his stick and deflected the puck. The guys knew then that it was meant to be. It was just a matter of time.

Regulation time ended with the score tied at one. The best thing we had going for us was that damned song they kept playing. The Islanders desperately wanted to sing that song going off the ice at the end of the game. We wanted to shove it back at them.

The winning goal came on one of those innocent plays, as is so often the case in overtime. Ian Turnbull was coming up the left side; I was coming up the right and shifting towards the middle. He fired a high pass that I had to knock down with my glove. There were three Islanders right around me, and the puck kept bouncing. Three players— Clark Gillies, Potvin and Dave Lewis— were all close enough to make the play, but each was thinking the other guy was going to make it. Having three guys there was probably the best thing that could have happened, because had there been only one, he would have taken me. Goalie Chico Resch came charging out of the net, and I let the shot go. I didn't get a hard shot away, but somehow, four minutes and thirteen seconds into overtime, a fluttering shot from a guy with a broken bone in his wrist and a broken nose became the winning goal.

The Leafs had beaten the Islanders. The only music we heard was our own. The Nassau Coliseum was in a silent state of shock.

Even after the goal went in, it took a long time to register that I had actually scored— that the series was over. It took me all the way from being 25 feet out, to skating past Resch, to circling the net before I finally thought, "My God, it's over." We sang ourselves silly that night, only to quickly come back to earth the next day. Next up were the Montreal Canadiens, who had won the last two Stanley Cups. They swept us out of the playoffs in four straight games

Everyone was so gung ho in Roger's first year, we were probably overachievers. The second year, the newness wore off a little. There is life outside the rink but sometimes Roger didn't seem to realize that. He was single, and hockey meant everything to him. Roger wanted the guys to spend all their time in the rink. Nevertheless, he was the best coach I had played for so far.

After we knocked off the Islanders, expectations for the Leafs were high as the 1978–79 season began— probably too high. Roger was disappointed; the team was disappointing. Much as we tried, we couldn't get back the same feeling we had when we beat the Islanders. As the season went on, Roger came under more and more pressure and was taking heat on behalf of the club. It all came to a head one March night in Montreal.

We lost to the Canadiens in Montreal, 1–0, and it was a terrific hockey game. Roger came in after the game and said, "I appreciate the kind of effort you guys have put in. It was a dream of mine to beat Scotty [Bowman], especially in his own building. Unfortunately, it didn't come true. And unfortunately, I've been relieved of my duties."

The dressing room was silent. Everyone was in shock. The instant reaction was, "I can't believe this has happened." After the shock wore off, the second reaction was, "We can't let this happen." The players felt partly responsible for all this because we weren't playing well at the time. But still, we knew one thing: If we were going to go anywhere in the playoffs, we needed Roger as our coach. It was too late in the season to bring in someone new. Besides, we didn't want another coach.

When we got back to Toronto that night, the players wanted to do something to fight the decision. The calls went back and forth until well into the night, and the next morning Darryl Sittler was at the arena, representing the players, to try to have Roger reinstated as coach. He went to see Harold Ballard and Jim Gregory. Ultimately, the decision was Harold's.

As players, we still didn't know what was going on. We didn't know if we had a coach or who the coach would be or what was in store for us for the rest of the season. Harold played this emotional situation for all it was worth: He wanted Roger to come out behind the bench during a game with a bag over his head, then remove the bag and let the fans see who he was. No matter what happened, it would be a fiasco. We really didn't know what was going to happen. That night, when the national anthem was played, there was no coach behind the Leafs bench. And then, at the very last minute, Roger walked out to his usual spot. I don't ever remember hearing that kind of standing ovation for a coach. And we were as fired up as the fans were.

Knowing Roger the way I do and knowing what a proud person he is, the whole situation was a real low point for him. Even though he had been reinstated and his heart was with the Maple Leafs, it was never the same. You don't just fire a guy and then rehire him and expect him to do the kind of work Roger did. He would spend all day at the rink doing the work that two or three coaches do today. And in a lot of cases, he did it better than a lot of them do it today.

After the dust had settled, it was playoff time. Our opening round matchup was a best-of-three series with the Atlanta Flames, the team I had almost been traded to a few seasons back. The Flames had finished nine points ahead of us in the standings, and we weren't expected to beat them. But we did. Rather easily, I might add. And Roger's coaching had a lot to do with it. Again, we ran into the Montreal Canadiens in the second round and again, we lost to the team that won the Stanley Cup. If there was any consolation, we thought

Roger's job would be saved because we beat the Flames and lost to the eventual champions. As it turned out, it didn't matter. Roger was let go, and he wasn't alone.

In the back of our minds, we were preparing ourselves for Roger to be fired. But it was a total shocker when Jim Gregory, the general manager, was also let go, especially knowing the kind of man he was and knowing how much he meant to the players. He was considered to be about as fair a GM as we'd known. And we were unhappy to be losing him.

That summer, rumours swirled until the Leaf job was finally filled. Toronto took a step into its past while looking towards it future when the Leafs hired Punch Imlach as general manager. We didn't know it then, but playing for the Maple Leafs would never be the same.

5

I WAS BORN
IN A
SMALL TOWN

I'd follow him anywhere.

It's one thing to be able to relate stories, but it's another matter entirely finding the right words to describe someone who means as much to me as my father does. To me, my dad was everything and to this day, my dad is still my hero. Now, just like then, I'd follow him anywhere if I could. As a kid I loved to be around him, and it's really no different now.

What I learned from him, more than anything else, was the value of hard work and honesty— and I can't think of anything more important to learn from a father. If there was work to be done, he didn't tell me to do it; he said, "Come on, let's go do it." Working together with my dad never seemed like a chore. I like to describe him as a man's man or the salt of the earth, but those descriptions both seem inadequate.

Our relationship was solidified when my mother returned to teaching full time and I stayed at home on the farm with Dad. My mom describes those days as an "oh-be-joyful arrangement, a father-and-son trust fund with high interest rates and boundless dividends." I spent two years tagging after Dad and "helping" with chores. When he worked in the fields, I was right beside him on the tractor. When he milked the cows, I held the buckets. When he fixed machinery, I advised. Looking back, I suppose I was more of a hindrance than a help, but I figured I was a big guy and certainly indispensable to running the farm! Those were times I'll never forget.

I was five and a half when I started school and just a few weeks older than that when I quit. One morning I got up and announced that I wasn't going to go anymore. School wasn't that great, and besides, Dad needed me to help with the chores. Mom and Dad didn't share my convictions about staying at home, and I was sent back to school. Still, I missed my dad.

Frank Orr, the hockey writer with *The Toronto Star*, used to kid me that when someone turned their toaster on in Craigmyle, the street lights dimmed. Shows how much those big-city guys know: Craigmyle didn't have street lights! I really *was* born in a small town and even went to a three-room country school through grade eight. And for three of those years, my mother was my teacher. I used to have to call her "Mrs. McDonald" when we were in school, and it drove me crazy. I was sure then that she picked on me and always tried to make an example of me. Now that I'm a parent, I recognize that I was testing her patience far more than she ever tested mine!

I may have been born in a small town, but I grew up a farm boy, and, like the song says, I wouldn't have it any other way. It was a childhood full of good times and hard work, full of learning from my folks about "first things first," about honesty, about determination, about learning how to make things "do" on a farm. It was a childhood full of a deep sense of family and community. We grew up in a spirit of togetherness and helping your neighbour.

In the country, neighbours are often more than people who live close to you: They're friends who show up when the going gets tough, and in the Hand Hills, a real community spirit prevailed. We'd all get together for brandings, butchering rings and carpentry bees and to get ready for the Hand Hills Stampede. If someone was behind with his harvesting, it wasn't uncommon for a full crew of neighbours—along with their machinery—to show up and help with the work. I remember one year when our combine broke down, and before the parts were in to fix it, the neighbours who had already finished their harvest arrived. We had six combines and trucks going all out, and before we knew it, our fields were done, and it was our turn to join the relay to the next farm. I even remember a time when my dad was sick with the mumps, and we'd promised to do chores for a neighbour who had gone away for a few days. Mom went out and dutifully did farm chores for the neighbours. After summer church services, most of the congregation would have a group picnic and then pick teams for baseball. Whatever the activity, we did it together!

Most of all, we learned the importance of family. Growing up on the farm, we didn't have a lot of material things, but we did have a rich family life. When a household is filled with love and warmth and caring, you don't need a whole lot more. Like farm families everywhere, we relied on each other for companionship and playmates. We were four children—two boys, two girls. I was the baby, but honest, I wasn't spoiled! Often, after chores, we'd play ball: My brother, Lynn, and I both liked to pitch, and Donna would always "volunteer" to be our catcher. Although she never complained, sometimes we played so long that her hands ended up black and blue. Once, when our favourite catcher was "missing in action," I talked my other sister into taking her place. I threw the ball too quickly and it broke Dixie's glasses, leaving her with two black eyes for a week. I just couldn't understand why she never wanted to play with us again! We also used to barrel race, and I'll never forget Mom and Dad laughing at the four of us kids as we tried to run on the rolling drums. We'd stand on top of a 45 gallon oil drum and try to roll it across the farmyard without falling off, kind of like lumberjacks doing log rolling. The game may have been great for developing balance, but it also developed lots of bruised knees and skinned shins. In the evenings, we'd recover from our wounds by gathering around the kitchen table with Mom and Dad and playing cards. Dad was either the best or the luckiest card player of the McDonald clan; and I'm still trying to top him in a game of whist or crib.

My mother, Phyllis, has a warm exuberant personality and was always there not only for her own family but for anyone who might need a helping hand or just a sympathetic ear. She was deeply involved with whatever community activity was going on. She played organ at church, organized concerts and school plays, taught art classes and worked with the Ladies Aid putting on showers and dances. We always kidded her about her "cooking disability" but I must admit we really didn't suffer. Even though she juggled a full schedule of family, friends and a full-time teaching job, I always knew that being a mom was the most important to her.

Lynn, who was four years older than me, was very good at sports, and I was always tagging along after him and his friends. I was younger and smaller and not as strong as the older kids, so I had to work twice as hard just to keep up most of the time; that's probably where I developed my competitive spirit. And I really have to thank Lynn for putting up with a tag-along. My attitude hasn't changed much since those farm days: I still feel you have to work hard to always keep that competitive edge.

Most kids grow up playing road hockey, but Lynn and I spent our spare time either shooting pucks in the basement or shooting them against the garage. Once in a while we'd even lose our bottle money after breaking a window! I think all that shooting developed my wrists; and it was in that basement and on the driveway that my wrist shot came to be.

One day I found out that I didn't have to be bigger or stronger than Lynn—just smarter! He always used to puff up his chest and challenge me, "Come on kid, give me your best shot." I'd wind up and plow him right in the chest; he'd hardly feel it, but it gave him an excuse to whale me. Well, one day he challenged me again, but this time I had it figured out. I looked him straight in the eye, wound up for my best haymaker and instead kicked him right square in the shin! He went down like a sack of bricks, and I ran like hell! He wasn't quick to challenge me the next time. His kid brother was learning.

I didn't always learn as quickly though. My sister, Donna, and I are two years apart, and we had our differences, as all brothers and sisters do. But what used to drive me crazy was that she was always making up the rules for whatever we were playing. It wasn't until I got a little bit older that I discovered that not everyone changes the rules part way through a game. We laugh about Donna's rules now, and she swears that I'm making up stories. But I have to remember that she is getting older, and her memory is probably failing. Donna has always worked hard for what she's accomplished; she's a very determined lady, and I admire her a lot.

When I was twelve, my sister Dixie had a new boyfriend, and I thought he was great. Don played hockey, so of course he was OK by me. I liked going to his games with Dixie, and I always thought going to them was my idea. But I remember my mother never objected to me tagging along with Dixie and Don; as a matter of fact, she was quite insistent that I go. Dixie and Don still tease me about being their chaperone. The nice part was they never treated me as if I were a kid brother—I felt more like a pal. And we still banter back and forth about those days and the good times we had.

One of the things I remember most from my childhood is looking back at the end of a day and seeing how much work we'd completed. Whether it was haying, cleaning corrals, picking rocks or summer fallowing, there's a real sense of accomplishment that goes with farm life and working as a family.

We all grew up in the Hand Hills—the heartland of Alberta—and from our living room window you can see forever—all the way down the valley to the Hand Hills Lake. It was there I learned to skate. I was five years old, and my first skates were two sizes too big, a pair of hand-me-downs from my brother. But I didn't care, I was skating, and I loved it! We lived on a hill two and a half miles above the school, and once I learned to skate I wanted to do it all the time. Sometimes I'd even walk down to the creek and skate my way over rough patches, smooth ice and even some grassy spots to get to school. It sure wasn't the Rideau Canal, and I wasn't Rocket Richard, but it got me there. The fathers in our school district built a rink beside our three-room school, and all winter we spent our phys. ed. periods, our lunch recess, any time we could, skating on our very own "arena." There was always a race to see who could get laced up first, to get as much skating time in as possible, and only a western Chinook could suspend our skating program.

At a very early age, I developed a love for hockey. There was romance in sitting around on a cold winter's night, listening to the living-room radio, with Foster Hewitt taking us to Maple Leaf Gardens and other NHL arenas. That seemed like sheer fantasy, but reality was just as captivating.

It was one thing to cheer like crazy for those far-away Maple Leafs, but it was another to actually be at a live hockey game. My real hero played for the Hand Hill Broncs of the No. 9 Hockey League. The league was named after the Alberta highway that connected the towns along that stretch. The Hanna Hornets and teams from Endiang and Sherness were among the league favourites. My hero then—as he is now—was Lorne McDonald, my dad. There is nothing I can remember that was more enjoyable than going to watch my dad play hockey. He played defence and loved to throw the big bodycheck or block a shot; I'm sure he stopped as many shots as the goalie did some nights. Dad would come home bruised and battered but with a grin from ear to ear.

The Hand Hills Broncs was one of the first teams I was ever part of. I started off as their water boy, but soon I graduated to tape boy and then to stick boy. The only problem was that I was so young, I couldn't see over the boards while standing beside the bench. I was probably the only stick boy to do his job from the stands. I used to sit in the second row behind the bench and hand the sticks down to the players who needed them. It was such fun being at the games and having my own team to take care of that it just might have been the greatest job I've ever had.

When I was six years old, I started playing organized hockey. We lived about 22 miles from Hanna, and it was a big deal for us to get in to town for practices and games. My dad had the farm to run, and my mom was a school teacher, but somehow they still found the hours to drive Lynn and me to town. Half of my time in minor hockey was spent in Hanna, the other half was spent in the car. I can't believe the number of miles my parents drove to keep us in hockey. They never pushed either of us, but they were always there to lend a supporting hand and give words of encouragement.

Some of the funniest memories I have from minor hockey are the days we used to go speeding down the gravel roads to get to the games, and all the while I'd be changing into my equipment in the car. I don't think I was ever early for a practice or a game, and more often than not, I was slightly late. Sometimes we'd be so late that I'd even put my skates on in the car, and my father would carry me into the rink and put me on the ice.

In my second year of minor hockey, a man named Ron Howery became my coach. He decided to start with the seven- and eight-year-olds and continue coaching us through the levels of minor hockey; Ron ended up coaching me from my "Mighty Mite" years all the way through the time when I left to play "Midget." Year in and year out, we knew what to expect from our coach, and he knew what we were capable of. You couldn't slack off with Ron— he wouldn't let you. More than that, you didn't want to let him down. Just knowing him made you want to work harder.

For me, every game we played was a road trip. Since Hanna was 22 miles from home, the games we played were even further away. I loved the road trips then: They were the times when you didn't have a care in the world except for hockey; and that was my life. Often, after a road trip, we'd arrive back in Hanna late at night, and I'd bunk in with one of my teammates in town. The Babbs, Bellises, Lampsons, McCraes and Taylors must have thought they'd adopted me, I was around so much!

Like my dad, I started my hockey career as a defenceman; but I was always caught rushing up-ice trying to score the big goal. My coaches thought it best to put me on a forward line, and there I've been ever since.

One highlight of my minor hockey came when I played for the Hanna Bantam Elks: We went through an entire season without losing a game and went on to win the Alberta championship with a victory over Cold Lake. There was a terrible blizzard on the day of one of the quarter-final games, and with our farm snowed in completely, we knew we'd never make it to the bus that was taking the team to Medicine Hat for the game. One of our neighbours called and said that if we could make it to his place, he could get me to town. My dad got out the tractor, and we crossed the fields to the Moench farm. Mr. Moench got his three-ton truck going, and we ploughed through the three- and four-foot drifts to the bus. We won, 17–3, and went on to the championships. Thank god for neighbours!

It was time for me to leave home: If I was ever going to make it in hockey, it had to be now. My friend, George McCrae, and I went to Lethbridge in 1969 to try out for the Sugar Kings, a tier-two team in the Alberta Junior Hockey League. We were a little nervous, but glad of the chance.

I made the team—incredible! From there, things were set up quickly: First, I registered for school at Winston Churchill, then I was sent to the sports store to get new skates. I was still wearing Lynn's hand-me-downs, and although I wasn't complaining, the trainer realized that I could probably perform better with skates that fit!

Later that same day, I met the family I'd be boarding with, and as soon as I met the Zsovans, Donna, John and ten-year-old Doug (the Gumper), I felt at home. I was only sixteen, and the Zsovans quickly became like a second family to me: They guided me through the rest of my growing-up years, encouraged my hockey (I still have the quarters that John gave me for every goal I scored) and helped me mature. With my first two paycheques from the Sugar Kings— a grand total of $15 a month over and above my room and board— the Zsovans and I went shopping. I needed an overcoat and also picked out three new shirts— green, blue and purple (my incredible sense of fashion developed early). The bill was $10 more than my paycheques, and John kicked in the rest. They really did treat me like a son. I can still taste Donna's cinnamon rolls, fresh out of the oven, and will always think of Gump as my little brother.

I was a little apprehensive about calling home. I made the call— collect— and told Mom and Dad that I'd made the team, registered at school and found a great place to live. Goodbye. I didn't want to give them a chance to say anything, in case they said I was too young to stay. The next day, without warning, Mom showed up in Lethbridge. To this day, I'm not sure if she came to take me home or to make sure everything was really all right!

That was Mom. Being a school teacher, she was concerned about my education, and although she realized that hockey meant a lot to me, she also knew that not everyone who wants to play in the NHL makes it.

I spent two years in Lethbridge and graduated from high school before I left. I sure remember the difference between the three-room school I was used to and a large high school. It wasn't easy playing hockey and keeping up with school work, but I had great support from a teacher named Cliff Daw. Mr. Daw was a friend to many of the students and a confidante who could always help you see the other side of a problem. I was honoured to share the podium with him when I gave the toast to the faculty at my graduation and he gave the reply.

I must admit, I almost didn't graduate. After the

hockey season was over, I decided to abandon the rest of grade twelve and go to work. The trainer for the Sugar Kings, Pete Vanderhilt, also owned a tar-and-gravel roofing company, and he reluctantly gave me my first job. He thought I should continue with my schooling, but he knew that I was determined to get out into the world and make some money. After a month on the job, Pete convinced me to return to school, take my departmental exams and graduate with my class. I'll always be grateful to Pete for that.

I certainly don't advocate others taking schooling for granted; even though I was allowed to go back and finish my grade twelve, I realized that I had gambled with my education. It made me recognize the value of even a high-school diploma, and I can't stress its importance enough to kids coming through the ranks. Many, of my teammates on the Flames have chosen to go the college route before playing pro; it gave them the opportunity to combine hockey with earning a degree. And the NHL is now drafting college players on a regular basis. But still, I think the Western Hockey League is Number 1!

The reality of a teenaged son leaving home wasn't easy for my parents. After all, I was the last to leave the nest. When I was still on the farm, my dad and I used to get up every morning and milk five cows. We always tease Dad by saying that when I left for Lethbridge, he turned the cows out to pasture and hasn't milked one since.

Living so far from town, it wasn't easy to run in for repairs when a piece of machinery broke down. We learned to improvise, to make do. And we always kidded my dad that he was able to fix anything with a pair of pliers and a bit of wire. Our machinery wasn't the newest, and he had lots of opportunities over the years to practise his pliers-and-wire tricks. After signing with the Maple Leafs, I bought him a new tractor, hoping to show him how much his support, encouragement and friendship meant to me. But he still wouldn't throw away his stash of wire—just in case!

6

GLORY
DAYS

Last I heard, John Senkpiel was running a business in British Columbia. John Senkpiel, you ask? Had it not been for him and a coach named Scotty Munro, my hockey career might have gone in an entirely different direction. This is a complicated story, the type of story that can only happen in junior jockey.

In 1970 I was playing for the tier-two Lethbridge Sugar Kings of the Alberta Junior Hockey League, which was a farm team of the Calgary Centennials of the Western Canada Junior Hockey League. Well, the Western Canada League was expanding, putting a franchise into Medicine Hat, Alberta, and the new club was allowed to pick players from each of the existing franchises. The Medicine Hat club, known as the Tigers, picked John Senkpiel from the Centennials. But the late Scotty Munro, coach of the Cents, talked Senkpiel into not reporting to Medicine Hat. It was an old trick of Scotty's, and as anyone will tell you, he was a pretty shrewd hockey man. He'd talk a player into not reporting to another team, then trade a less valuable player to the team instead. Scotty didn't want to lose someone off his regular roster, so instead, he offered Medicine Hat the choice of any player from his Lethbridge farm team— any player except goaltender John Davidson. The Medicine Hat Tigers chose me. The rest, as they say, is history.

At first, I didn't report to the Tigers, and it had nothing to do with hockey. I was going to high school in Lethbridge and wanted to graduate before I moved on to play major junior. I'm glad I did it that way, because I finished school and also wound up as the AJHL's most valuable player in 1970-71, which gave me the confidence I needed to move up the ladder. My dream was one step closer.

In Lethbridge, as in Toronto, it took time before I found my comfort zone. My first year, I scored three goals, and I seriously doubted if I was going anywhere in hockey. We had travelled to Edmonton to play back-to-back games against the Movers and the Maple Leafs, the two Edmonton teams in the AJHL. Nothing went right that weekend, and on the bus ride home, I got to thinking that I just wasn't cut out for this life. And, sitting in the back of the Lethbridge Sugar Kings' bus, I started to cry. I've always been somewhat emotional, and this was just one of those times when my confidence failed me, one of those times when the game got the best of me, and it was difficult to overcome.

Still, I was fortunate. I learned more about hockey in my years of playing with the Sugar Kings than I probably learned anywhere else, and there was one reason why. His name is John Chapman, and although he's never coached in the NHL, he's sent a pretty impressive delegation of players in that direction: five Sutter brothers, John Davidson, Randy and Mike Moller, Dave Barr, Danny Gare, Mike Rogers and Ken Wregget. And with that, I'm sure I'm forgetting more than I'm remembering.

It seemed to me that Chapman always related to the guys who were willing to give it their best. You look at the list of guys he's turned pro, and you realize that they have one common characteristic— they may not be the most talented guys in the world, but they are guys who are willing to pay the price. Chappy learned his hockey in the old Eastern League and got by on giving it his all, every game.

He had a way of getting his message across. More than anything else, Chappy instilled a fear in his players: If you didn't want to give it 100 percent, he didn't want you on his team. I remember a few games where we hadn't played well or we'd lost. As soon as the stands were empty, he had us right back out on the ice practising. He wanted to be a winner, and he wanted us to be winners. And there's nothing wrong with that.

Chappy has won Centennial Cups (tier-two national championships) and Western League championships, but he's never moved to the NHL, although he's certainly capable. He's still coaching in the Western Junior League, and as always, doing a fine job.

If I am grateful to Chappy for what he taught me about effort and desire, I'm also grateful to a coach named Jack Shupe. People don't remember this, but I was a centreman until I joined the Medicine Hat Tigers. In fact, I played centre after I reported to the Tigers, but not for long. My first season in Medicine Hat, I began as the Number 3 centre, behind Stan Weir and Tom Lysiak, which isn't bad company to be in. After a few games at centre, Jack asked the three of us if one of us would like to play the wing. More specifically, he asked

me if would like play right wing with Lysiak. I had
played wing before—with George McRae, a friend of
mine who had originally taken me to Lethbridge. At
first, I was a little apprehensive, but once I considered
all the possibilities, I went along with it.

It was the best move anyone ever asked me to make.
No matter how hard I try, I can't picture myself as a
successful centre in the NHL. I wonder, had I not been
moved to right wing, how it all would have turned out.

Life in junior hockey with Lysiak and the Medicine
Hat Tigers was like a fantasy come true. A man once
told me a little secret. He said to make sure you really
enjoy yourself when you're playing junior hockey because when you turn pro, it's still fun, but it becomes a
job, too. That man was Glen Sather, and at the time I
was working at the Glen Sather Hockey School in Banff.
Sather was right; there was something fresh, something
exciting about playing in the Western Canada Hockey
League—which to me, then, meant I had made the big
time.

The old Western League, which has since been
renamed the Western Hockey League, was full of
characters in those days. Scotty Munro ran the Calgary
franchise, and his attitude about publicity was that you
could say anything you wanted about him, as long as
you spelled his name right. I've always thought that
when you're as successful and as highly thought of as
Scotty was, you deserve at least that! Brian Shaw, with
the Edmonton Oil Kings, was known for his wardrobe.
Now, Brian always thought he was in style, but when he
was dancing on the top of the players' bench and yelling
at the refs, you had trouble telling which was louder—
his voice or his jacket! But the real voice of the Edmonton organization was Wild Bill Hunter, who could be
found bellowing from the press box. This was the same
"Wild Bill" who tried in vain years later to move the St.
Louis Blues to Saskatoon. Paddy Ginnell was running

the Flin Flon team like a military camp. You always knew his boys by their brush cuts and the fire in their eyes. The New Westminster Bruins on the coast had Ernie (Punch) MacLean, and they didn't call him Punch for nothing. Nor were his teams afraid to live up to his nickname.

In Medicine Hat, we were the new kids on the block, and our franchise was owned by three successful businessmen in our community: George Maser, Rod Carry and Joe Fisher. These gentlemen set a high standard of operation and treated their players as men, something owners don't always do when dealing with junior players. In Medicine Hat, we were also different: We had the greatest fans in the league! The arena held 4000 people, but there were seldom less than 5200 people at a game (don't tell the fire marshal). Each one of them was cheering wildly for "their" boys, and I know our success was due in no small part to the support of our loyal fans.

As an expansion team, we had acquired guys from all over the league, but we had no shortage of talent. If there was one thing our coach, Jack Shupe, knew about, it was talent. Not only did Jack understand his players, but he got the best out of them. Starting from scratch, it took him only three seasons to build a team that won a berth in the Memorial Cup, Canada's junior hockey championships.

My beginnings in Medicine Hat were like my beginnings just about anywhere else. Unimpressive. I've come to the conclusion that I may not be a great starter, but I usually finish well. I wasn't playing great at centre when they moved me to the wing, and it took me a while before I adjusted to playing on a line with Lysiak and Derek Kuntz. But once everything fell into place, the world changed.

Sometimes you get placed with an unselfish and marvellously talented player like Lysiak, and it becomes magic, everything clicks! That's the way it was with us: Everything seemed to work. Years later, he reminded me a lot of Darryl Sittler. The two were basically the same kind of player. They would do anything to win, and when the game started, they were ready to play. And both didn't care who got the goal—you or them—just as long as someone scored.

Because of our success together in junior, the names Lysiak and McDonald would be linked together for a long time. We were good friends, but very different people. Our pro careers, while both successful, were also very different. Maybe it had to do with the fact that I wound up in Toronto and he went to Atlanta. But I think some of it had to do with the quiet confidence Tommy had, a confidence he carried right onto the Flames' team. His adjustment period in the league was one game. Mine was two years. But in the end, though, I think I appreciated success more than I would have had I not experienced the difficult years first.

Our final year of junior was 1972, the year of the famed Canada–Russia hockey series. Everyone, of course, remembers the Paul Henderson goal that won the series for Team Canada. But not many people remember the World Cup of Hockey, just three months after the famed Summit Series. There may be a good reason no one remembers it: Canada didn't win.

It was actually a four-country tournament played in the United States, and the Medicine Hat Tigers were chosen to represent Canada. The United States sent their usual hard-working team. The Czechs sent a majority of their national team, and the Soviets presented virtually the same lineup that had played stride for stride with the NHL's best.

After Team Canada beat the Soviets in September, we thought it was only right that we become the next team to do so. It wasn't just the Medicine Hat Tigers against the Russians. It was Canada vs. Russia! We bolstered our regular lineup for the tournament with John Davidson, the goalie from Calgary, Dennis Sobchuk, from Regina, and Vic Mercredi, from New West. We started the tournament with a game against the Czechs, and optimists that we were, we actually thought we had a chance to beat them. It was a reasonably close game until the third period, when they scored a couple of quick goals, and we lost, 5-1. We thought, "Hey, we're not so bad." In our game against the Russians, we found out we were. Compared to them.

We played the Soviets at the Met Center in Bloomington, the home of the Minnesota North Stars. That Soviet club had Vladislav Tretiak as their goalie, Alexander (Rags) Ragulin on defence and Valery Kharlamov, Alexander Yakushev and Boris Mikhailov among the forwards. We were in big trouble!

To give you an indication of how badly we were outplayed, we were down 8-0 two minutes into the second period. They were awesome. It was then that Jack Shupe mercifully replaced Sam Clegg in goal and let Davidson see what he could do. Davidson played the final 38 minutes, allowed only four goals against and was voted Canada's player of the game.

We were so overwhelmed by the Soviets that we didn't even notice that they had taken Tretiak out for part of the game. For all we know, he wasn't even dressed for the third period! They put another goalie in net and put their third goaltender on the bench wearing Tretiak's jersey. Those Russians gave us a lesson in hockey: Speed, fitness, puck control and team work— they could do it all. They ended up beating us 12-4. It was my first taste of international hockey, and despite the result, I knew I wanted more.

To be perfectly honest, I don't remember what happened in our game with the United States. I do remember the Czech game well. And I remember the Soviet game. But I just don't know what happened in our game against the States.

American players hadn't carved their niche in the NHL then as they have today, and we really didn't look upon their team as a threat to our position. In fact, until I pulled the old program out of a trunk in the basement, I didn't even realize that Bob Johnson, my coach with the Calgary Flames, was coaching the American team at that tournament. Maybe I should change my story and say I remember the US game vividly but I even had to ask Bob who won the game! He told me that it ended with a 4–4 tie, but I wonder if he's really telling the truth....

I do remember what happened after our game with the Soviets. Of all the Soviet players then, perhaps the most legendary was Alexander Ragulin, the defence-man. After the game, the Tigers went across the street to the Marriott Hotel, where we were staying, and crowded into a room discussing the tournament. The Russian team was celebrating in another room, drinking vodka. A couple of the guys in our room were having an arm wrestling "championship" when in walked Ragulin. In sign language he let us know that he wanted to take on Jim McCrimmon in arm wrestling.

Now, Jimmy McCrimmon is no weakling. I think he weighed about 220 pounds then and was one of the strongest and toughest guys in the WCHL. The two sat down together, tried each other's wrists out, then began. Before anyone could even say "go," Ragulin snapped Jimmy's wrist down like it was nothing. They both stood up, with Jimmy congratulating Ragulin. Just to show his real strength, the Russian picked Mc-Crimmon up and threw him across the room. Jimmy flew so far that he actually sailed across the bed and onto the floor.

Everyone just stood there, staring in open-mouthed

amazement. Jimmy got up saying very politely, "Thank you very much, thank you very much, thank you..." We really realized then just how strong the Soviets were, and it was a total shock.

After the tournament, it was back to the regular life of the WCHL. And our season ended well. The team won the league. Tommy won the scoring title and the most-valuable player award. I finished third in league scoring and made the league's first all-star team. We were on our way to Montreal to win the Memorial Cup. But we ran into one problem: We didn't win.

I don't know how many times I've played that Memorial Cup over in my head, and I still consider what happened to be a shame. Three teams played off for the Canadian Junior Championship— Medicine Hat Tigers, Toronto Marlies and Quebec Remparts. The Marlies were considered the favourites going in, but we beat them 3–2 in the first game of the tournament. Then the Marlies, as expected, beat Quebec. To reach the one-game final, we didn't even have to beat the Remparts. If we lost by two goals, we still would have played for the championship.

This Memorial Cup was different than most. For starters, it was played in Montreal, just a few days prior to the NHL draft, which was held there. Memorial Cups are the final showcase for the graduating juniors. This Cup was no different, especially considering that some of the top-ranked juniors were getting their last chance to show something. Five of the top-ranked players— Lysiak, John Davidson, who we had picked up as our goaltender, Andre Savard of Quebec, Bob Dailey of the Marlies and myself— were in the tournament, and need-less to say, the media hype was incredible. There was more talk about the draft than there was about the games.

I don't think it was intentional, but as players, we probably let our minds wander more than we should have. There was so much going on, and we were too easily distracted. As things turned out, we lost 7–4 to Quebec, and the stars of that team were Savard and Guy Chouinard, the same Guy Chouinard who I've enjoyed success with while playing for the Flames. Guy and I have laughed about that game once or twice over the years. Actually, he's laughed. I still don't find it all that funny. Guy has a picture of that game, with him scoring a goal. In the photograph, both Bob Gassoff and myself had gone down to block the shot, but without success. Guy likes to tell the story that after knocking us both down, he scored. The funny thing is, knowing Guy as well as I do, if he knocked us both down to score that goal, we were probably his first— and last— hits! Right, Guy?

After losing to Quebec, and thus being eliminated, we had no choice but to watch the final game. We were miserable. The Marlies won easily; I think the score was 9–1. It was unbelievably frustrating sitting in the stands watching, knowing full well we should have been playing. I'll hand it to the Marlies: With Mike Palmateer in goal, the Howe brothers, Mark and Marty, Bob Dailey and Paulin Bordeleau, they had an awfully good club. But I still feel we could have beaten them. It's too bad we didn't get the chance.

Once the Memorial Cup ended, most of our team headed home. Lysiak, Gassoff and myself remained in Montreal, waiting for the draft day. Being drafted is strange. All week long you hear about who's going to pick you and why, but there's a feeling involved that's difficult to explain. Despite all you hear, you don't believe anything until it's done.

I remember waiting as the names were picked. The New York Islanders chose Denis Potvin. No real surprise— he was considered the best. The Atlanta Flames picked Tommy Lysiak, and he couldn't have been happier. The Vancouver Canucks, uncommitted before the draft, picked Dennis Ververgaert. Then the Toronto Maple Leafs made their choice.

I was listening to hear my name. I heard it called, but I somehow couldn't believe it. It had been my dream for so long, and now it was true. The Maples Leafs draft, Lanny McDonald from the Medicine Hat Tigers. You know you're supposed to move, but nothing seems to work. I sat there like I was in a fog. Stan Obodiac, the Leafs amiable public relations man, walked with me toward the Toronto table at the draft, where I met Jim Gregory and King Clancy. Harold Ballard wasn't there—he was off on a sabbatical of sorts. "Sit right here, sonny," King Clancy said to me. I was shaking hands with a legend, my dream was unfolding. So much was happening so fast.

The most comforting face at the Maple Leaf's table belonged to a man named Torchy Schell. Torchy was a scout with the Maple Leafs, a guy who had taken a great interest in me in my final seasons of junior. Often he would take me aside and tell me little things he thought might improve my game. Torchy had a warmth about him, and knowing he cared made me work that little bit harder to earn his approval. He was always helpful and a good friend, and I was always grateful. I remember one night in Saskatoon during my final year playing for the Tigers, when Torchy and Johnny Bower, another Leafs scout, took me out for dinner after the game. I didn't consider that I was out with Johnny Bower, Leafs' scout. As far as I was concerned, I was out for dinner with Johnny Bower, all-time great Leafs' goaltender, and that was first rate! The Leafs' main backstop for those glory years was taking the time to give me a few pointers. Whatever happened after that was a bonus; I couldn't wait to tell my Dad that I'd actually had dinner with Johnny Bower!

Scouts are supposed to find players, but in the case of Torchy Schell, I can think of one player he saved—

me. When I first joined the Leafs, I was having all kinds of trouble skating. To be more specific, I spent almost as much time lying on the ice as I did skating on it. I just couldn't seem to feel secure on my skates, no matter what I did.

Torchy, knowing that I had never had this problem before, paid a visit to Lou Klachinsky, our trainer in Medicine Hat. Lou was one of those guys who had been around hockey all his life and was almost like an assistant coach is today, a buffer between the players and the coach. Lou was just an all-round great guy, and he often kidded me that I wasn't a pretty skater. He was probably right. Anyway, Torchy asked Lou what he thought was wrong, and Lou told him it looked like I was falling down because there wasn't enough blade on the ice.

It turned out that Guy Kinnear, the Leafs' trainer, was putting too much rocker on my skates—which is how most players prefer it—leaving as little blade as possible on the ice. Lou told Torchy to get Guy to change the blade on my skates, and suddenly one of my problems disappeared.

I was fortunate for a lot of reasons in junior hockey. Fortunate to play for coaches like John Chapman and Jack Shupe. Fortunate that I was moved from centre to right wing, that I got to play in a World Cup and a Memorial Cup and that people like Torchy Schell and Lou Klachinsky cared.

I was also fortunate in another area: today's system of drafting eighteen-year-olds wasn't around in 1973. I was twenty-two years old before my pro career began to blossom, and if I'd been drafted at eighteen, I don't think I'd be in a position to be writing this book today.

7

INTERNATIONAL AFFAIRS

At first I thought it was Darryl Sittler on the phone playing a practical joke. The speaker claimed to be Alan Eagleson and said he wanted me to try out for Team Canada in preparation for the first Canada Cup tournament in 1976. I was convinced it was all a joke. Me? Playing for Canada? In the first Canada Cup? It took Eagle some talking, which he's naturally good at, to convince me that it was in fact him on the phone and that I was in fact being invited to Team Canada's training camp.

Playing for Team Canada then was a little different than it is now. Everytime you look around today, someone is playing someone else in international hockey. But this was the first Canada Cup tournament, and the first major opportunity since the Summit Series of 1972 for the best Canadian players to play the Soviets for a championship. And they wanted me to try out! I was ecstatic!

Eagleson cautioned me on the phone. Yes, be excited, but no, you haven't made the team yet. My first reaction had been, "Why would they want me?" And my second reaction was, "I think I have a good shot at making the team!"

This wasn't just an ordinary team. No team is ordinary when it has Bobby Orr on defence, not to mention Larry Robinson, Denis Potvin, Guy Lapointe and Serge Savard. I'm convinced each one of them will wind up in the Hockey Hall of Fame. No team is ordinary when it has Phil Esposito, Bobby Hull, Guy Lafleur, Gil Perreault, Marcel Dionne and Bobby Clarke at forward. It wasn't difficult to see why I was excited. I had only played three seasons in the NHL and had experienced only one good season. So when training camp began I was keyed up, and with good reason.

Our training camp in Montreal was very emotional. Everyone was working hard under our coaches— Scotty Bowman, Al MacNeil, Don Cherry and Bobby Kromm— and as Eagleson had warned me, we were battling for jobs. The last thing I needed was another controversy.

In a scrimmage game during camp, I hit Serge Savard with a hard, clean bodycheck. The Montreal Canadiens' star defenceman had always had problems with his legs, and when I hit him, he wrenched his knee. He turned around and two-handed me with his stick. There was some pushing and shoving and a few words exchanged, but it was just one of those heat-of-the-moment things. Our guys were all yelling to forget it, that we were a team, and I thought it was forgotten.

All I can say is that it's a good thing I can't read French. The French language press in Montreal, always looking for something controversial, decided that I had deliberately attempted to injure Savard, and I don't think he deterred them in any way. The newspapers were trying to build it into something it wasn't, and I refused to get involved. I was just there to do my best, and I could do so without hurting anyone else's chances.

While Savard and the French press may have been against me, others were on my side—Bobby Clarke to name one. He told me that it had been a great check, the kind of checking we'd have to use to win the tournament. The English press, including the respected Montreal hockey writer, Red Fisher, thought it was just part of the game. Still I was feeling a little insecure about things until Don Cherry said something to me.

"If you're going to make this club, those are the kind of checks you're going to have to make. I don't ever want to see you circling or swinging by a guy on the boards, because if you do, they'll take advantage."

The checking incident quieted down, and once we got back into the training camp routine, it was forgotten. I never joked about it with Serge, though. I never got to know Serge well enough to know if you can joke with him.

Like any other training camp, you keep a depth chart in your head. In camp I was playing right wing on a line with Darryl Sittler and Bob Gainey—not a bad line to be working with. Still, in the back of your mind, you're always counting. The numbers game, they call it. How many right wingers are in camp? How many are they keeping? There were six right wingers in camp, and in my mind I had conceded two spots already. No one was going to beat out Guy Lafleur, who led the NHL in scoring that season. And I didn't think anyone would beat out Reggie Leach of Philadelphia, who had scored 61 goals the previous season. That left four of us battling for two spots: Danny Gare and Rene Robert, both of whom played for Buffalo, Jean Pronovost from the

Pittsburgh Penguins and myself. Pronovost had scored 52 goals that season, Gare had 50, Robert's "French Connection" linemates, Gil Perreault and Rick Martin, were at the camp so I knew it would be tough.

Still, I thought I could make it. Even if I didn't make it, I knew I had been involved in one of the greatest experiences of my life. I probably learned more about hockey in that short time than in any other period. Each line had an off-ice coach, and ours was the Montreal Canadiens' legend, Toe Blake. Toe may not have been a man of many words, but when he did say something, you listened! One pointer from Toe was worth its weight in gold, or in goals! He understood the game as well as anybody I've ever talked to, and we couldn't have been more fortunate in having him as our advisor.

Camp was nearing its end, and cutdown day was approaching. It came after an exhibition game in Ottawa, and I don't think I'll ever forget walking out of that room. I had made the active list, and I just wanted to yell "yahoo." If this were all a dream, I didn't ever want to wake up. Darryl told me to stay calm and see what happened next. Even though I had beaten out Jean Pronovost and Rene Robert for a place on right wing, we were still carrying extra forwards.

My excitement at making the team was briefly put on hold. I didn't play the first two games, and Canada won them both. I understood why I wasn't playing. Most of the other players were older, more experienced and better known. It was only my third year, and my first good year. But still, I wanted to play.

The opportunity finally came in the third game of the six-team tournament. We were playing Sweden at Maple Leaf Gardens, and it was exciting. It felt good to be playing at the Gardens, coming back to represent my country, but I was nervous too. I knew that if I didn't perform well, I wouldn't get another chance.

Before the game we were introduced individually, and Darryl and I, being Maple Leafs players, got big ovations. But the largest ovation annoyed some members of Team Canada. Another Leaf, Borje Salming, was playing for Team Sweden, and he got an incredible welcome from the Gardens fans. Those of us who played with Borje understood. Many of the others didn't.

Our game plan, not coincidentally, was centred around Salming. We were told to bump him as much as we could. We used to kid Borje about being the King of Sweden, and often he played like he was the King of Hockey. Borje could control a game or turn it around, all by himself. No one knew that better than Darryl and I, and our game plan that night worked to perfection. We shut out Sweden.

Adjusting to international hockey isn't always easy. Here we were, top scorers from most of the NHL teams, together for a short period of time and asked to become a team. With the Leafs I was expected to score, but with Team Canada I didn't care what I had to do as long I got to play. Whatever they wanted me to do, I would do. I think if they had told me to play goal, I would have considered that too, although that might have been stretching commitment just a little far!

For Team Canada, I was a role player. There were other people there to do the scoring. Early in the Sweden game, I missed a check, and Grapes made sure I heard about it. "Look, that guy is going to be standing on the point all day long," he said to me. "If you run over him once, he won't be there any more." They wanted me to help give the team a physical presence, and Don Cherry made sure I knew my role. From that point on, I played a more physical role. I realized what I was there to do.

Being involved with this version of Team Canada was truly a treat. I was like a little kid, in awe of my teammates. When you looked around the dressing room and saw some of the greatest players to ever be in the hockey world, it's exciting. Talk about changing your style: In the Maple Leafs' dressing room, they couldn't shut me up; in the Team Canada dressing room, I only spoke when spoken to.

Playing with Sittler was, of course, enjoyable. But having the opportunity to play with Gainey was also special. There isn't a right winger in the NHL who wouldn't prefer to line up with Bob Gainey instead of against him. Gainey, in my mind, is the ultimate left winger. He can skate and shoot, and for the shot he's got, it's surprising he hasn't scored more goals than he has. A lot has to do with the fact that he's always lined up against the other team's top right winger. What makes Gainey so tough is not only that he can skate and shoot, but that he's big and strong and lanky. Just having the chance to play with him was truly a treat.

The Canada Cup was expected to come to a show-down between Team Canada and the Soviet Union, but it didn't work out that way. The Czechs surprised the Soviets in their match and won the game. And, in one of the greatest games ever played, we lost to the Czechs, 1-0. The pressure was on in the final game of the round-robin: If we lost, the Soviets would play the Czechs for "our" Canada Cup.

I don't remember ever being involved in a more exciting game than the 1-0 game with Czechoslovakia. Both teams played well. Both goaltenders, Rogie Vachon for Canada and Vladimir Dzurilla for the Czechs, were unbelievable. Our job in that game was to shut down the Czechs top line centred by Milan Novy, who later played for Washington. Well, Novy wound up scoring the game's only goal. At that point, our line vowed we wouldn't have another goal scored against us for the rest of the tournament. I don't know if we were scored against again, but it was that kind of commitment that made the tournament distinctive.

Playing in the NHL is one thing, with its own kind of excitement. But there's nothing to compare to the thrill of playing for your country. I don't know what it is: Beating the Islanders was exciting, beating the Oilers was unbelievable, getting to the Stanley Cup finals was a dream, but it's a different kind of excitement when you play for Canada. You carry that red Maple Leaf with pride.

After losing to the Czechs 1–0 in the round-robin, we were apprehensive heading into the best of three final against them. That is, we were at first. We won the first game, 6–0. I think the Czechs were so relieved to be in the finals instead of the Russians, they didn't really care that first game. But, in the second game, they played with the same enthusiasm of their earlier games. Some people might have thought it was going to be easy, but it wasn't.

Playing for Scotty Bowman was certainly an adjustment for some players, especially those used to skating on the same line all the time. Scotty liked to shake things up a little bit, and make no mistake, there were four coaches but this was Scotty's team. He was a legend by then, and he was in high gear. He knew what he was doing, and we listened.

Scotty had tried different left wingers with Darryl and me in the game against the Soviets. Sometimes Bob Gainey played with us, sometimes it was Perreault. For a while, Esposito centred our line and Darryl moved to left wing. In the third period of the final game against Czechoslovakia, Marcel Dionne was our centre.

It was a difficult game and we were trailing by a goal until Bill Barber scored late in the third period, putting it into overtime. Scotty's theory on overtime was to be smart but aggressive. "Don't sit back," he told us. He wanted to win the game outright, instead of just playing to prevent a goal being scored.

Before the overtime, Grapes came down from the

press box where he was spotting the game and told us that Dzurilla, the Czech goalie, was over-challenging. "If you get a chance," he said, "fake a shot and see what happens." As it turned out, Grapes knew what he was talking about!

Canada's tournament-winning goal was touched by all five skaters on the ice. The puck went from Larry Robinson to Denis Potvin, up the boards to me, and I threw it straight up centre to Dionne, who one-touched it to Sittler, who was breaking down the wing. Sittler had a step on the defenceman, and at the top of the faceoff circle, he faked a shot just like Grapes said, took one step sideways and shot the puck into the open net. Dzurilla had overcommitted. Team Canada won the Canada Cup. Pandemonium reigned. If there's another feeling like that, I'd sure like to find it; I don't ever remember being so excited.

Probably the most poignant moment of the whole tournament came at the end of that game. The Canada Cup had been presented and we stood shoulder to shoulder at the blue line watching as they raised the flag, the sounds of *O Canada* filling the Forum.

Replacing the traditional post-game handshake was something much more meaningful. I don't know who started it, but it was one of the great moments of sport. The teams crossed the ice and exchanged game sweaters, each acknowledging the contributions of the others to a fine series. For that brief moment in time, the politics of the world let down its guard.

It was especially sweet for me. No one really expected me to be there, and few expected me to be there when the final bell rang. And to be part of the winning goal.... Well, I knew then that my career had definitely turned around.

Another memory from that series: After our victory, Prime Minister and Mrs. Trudeau hosted a cocktail party at their home for the members of Team Canada and their wives. It was followed by a dinner at Government House to celebrate our winning the Canada Cup. That was my first taste of major international hockey. It wasn't my last, although it certainly was the best.

I was chosen to play in the ill-fated Challenge Cup series in 1979. It wasn't thought of as ill-fated then, it only came to be so after it was played. The Challenge Cup was different from the Canada Cup. It was something like Rendez Vous '87, except that instead of being two games against the Soviet Union, it was a best of three series.

Again, our team was strong. We had the usual array of great players: Dionne, Lafleur, Robinson, Dryden and Potvin; and by then Bryan Trottier and Mike Bossy had come into their own as two of hockey's best players. The Challenge Cup was played that year instead of the NHL's all-star game. We arrived in New York and had only two days of practice in preparation. Then we played three games in four days.

Although we weren't quite sure what to expect, we won the first game. After that, a quiet confidence set in, but it didn't last long. We lost the second game and suddenly the feeling was "My God, we could actually lose this series." It was one of those everything-to-lose situations. If we won, it didn't mean anything, because we were expected to win. If we lost, suddenly it was a black mark on the NHL and on us. Here we were, guys from all different clubs, expected to show up and become a representative team. It didn't work out that way, and you would think that the NHL would have learned something by now.

We knew how talented the Soviets were, but still they surprised us. Not with their ability to play hockey, but with their ability to adjust. We planned to play standard North American dump-and-chase hockey against them, hoping that, as in the past, they would have difficulty playing that style. This time, again with Scotty Bowman coaching, it didn't work out as well.

It used to be that when you played a Soviet team, they would always be circling around instead of going forward. Suddenly in the second game of the Challenge Cup series, they were the ones dumping the puck in and we were the ones who couldn't adjust. The Soviets were playing our game and we were playing ragged. Ken Dryden had won the first game in goal, and lost the second. The coaching staff decided to make a change for the third game.

Gerry Cheevers was a very different goalie from Dryden. Dryden was a standup, angle goaltender who played the basic style better than anyone else. Cheevers was a reflex goaltender, depending more on reaction and less on science. The coaches felt that an angle goalie like Dryden wasn't perfectly suited to play against the Soviets because of the tendency to make one extra pass. So, for the third game of the series, Cheevers was in the net, and we lost 6–0. Not that you can blame Cheevers; I really don't think that anything we could have tried would have worked that night.

We went back to our respective NHL teams, not exactly disgraced, but not enriched by the experience either. We left with a realization that the Soviets were changing. Not only were they willing and able to adapt their game, but, for the first time in my experience, they were playing with emotion. Previously, when they scored, they treated it as something expected— it was no big deal. Now it seemed you could see that scoring a goal meant something to them.

They've changed and the game has changed. The NHL has adopted a more European approach to hockey, and the Soviet game is more like the NHL than it was before. Now you see the Soviets shooting from the point on the power play, which they never attempted before. You see their defencemen pinching in more and going for the holes more than ever before. They can play our game now, and I think we can play theirs.

The only thing a series like the Challenge Cup proved is that you can't take a collection of hockey players, give them two days to practise together and expect them to be a team. Hockey doesn't work that way.

If the Canada Cup was an incredible experience and the Challenge Cup an eye-opening experience, then the World Championships were an experience of some kind... although I'm not quite sure what kind! I must confess that when I played for the Colorado Rockies, I sometimes looked forward to the end of a season. With months to go in a season, and knowing that we weren't going to challenge for Lord Stanley's Cup, many of us hoped to be picked to go overseas representing Canada at the World Championships. You'd think the last thing most people would feel like doing after playing a full season with the Colorado Rockies was playing more hockey. But some of us, I guess, were just plain crazy or something.

The best of the worst—that's what Canada sent to the Worlds. Not exactly a team of NHL misfits, but a team of the best players from teams that don't qualify for the playoffs. I've been asked to play for Canada three times at the World tournament, and twice I've had to say no because of injuries. But in 1981, after my first full season with the Rockies, I played for Canada in Göteborg, Sweden, and for the third time in my career, I was playing for coach Don Cherry.

Playing for Canada at the World Championships is different than playing for Canada at any other time. For starters, there are no big expectations and pressures. Canada isn't expecting you to win. But when you leave, the Canadian team still thinks that it's the one who will bring home the gold medal.

The Team Canada I played for in 1981 wasn't exactly the Challenge Cup or Canada Cup roster. Instead of

Dryden or Vachon in goal, we had John Garrett and Phil Myre. Instead of Orr and Potvin on defence, we had Norm Barnes, Dave Babych, Barry Long, Willie Huber, Rob Ramage and Rick Green. The best of the forwards were Mike Gartner, Dennis Maruk, John Ogrodnick, Mike Rogers and Steve Tambellini. We were the Colorado Rockies of the World tournament and Grapes was again coaching.

When we first got to Sweden, we noticed a definite difference between life overseas and life in the NHL. The food wasn't as good. Nor were the hotels. The beds were short and narrow, difficult to sleep on. Can you imagine six-foot five Willie Huber in a tiny bed? It wasn't a pretty sight! Still, there were things to enjoy. I liked playing on the big ice surface. I enjoyed the chance to do some sight-seeing. But it was disappointing to come home empty-handed, without a medal. Our highlight on the ice was a 4–4 tie against the Soviets. But as always, Grapes made it fun to play, win or lose.

During the tournament we followed the Stanley Cup playoffs at home. That was the year the Edmonton Oilers knocked off the Montreal Canadiens in the first round of the playoffs, and what that meant to us in Sweden was that we were getting reinforcements. Our lineup was strengthened by the addition of Larry Robinson and Guy Lafleur, who were going to make life somewhat easier for us even if they couldn't solve all our problems.

We were excited to be getting Robinson and Lafleur, but no one was more excited than Lucien DeBlois, a teammate of mine with the Rockies. Lafleur was Lucien's hero. When Lucien found out Lafleur was coming to Sweden to join the team, he couldn't stop talking about it. So as a favour to Lucien, Grapes put him on a line with Lafleur to start off the game against Holland. Well, the game had just begun when some Canadian playing for Holland hit Lafleur with a hell of a check in open ice. Guy had been forced to wear a helmet for the first time in this tournament, in keeping with international rules, and I don't know if he couldn't see properly or what, but this guy caught him unawares. That was it for Lafleur in the tournament. No one felt worse about it than Lucien, who lasted one shift on his hero's line.

We didn't win anything in Sweden, but we did have some fun. When you're overseas at a tournament like that, all you have is your team and you become a close group. When you're playing on foreign ice, with foreign referees, you feel like everyone is against you and it turned out they were.

If I were ever asked to represent Canada again at a World Championship, all things being equal, I'd say yes. I just hope I don't get asked, because that would mean we'd been eliminated from the playoffs early.

8

VINTAGE GRAPES

Lanny McDonald of the Colorado Rockies? No matter how many times I said it, it still didn't sound right. And it certainly didn't feel right.

At first I considered not reporting to the Rockies. It wasn't that I was considering quitting, I just wanted to put my career on hold while the rest of my life caught up. We were about to have our second child, and I was still in shock from being traded for the first time. Too much was happening too fast and I wanted the world to slow down. I wanted to be able to put everything into perspective. I kept thinking, "I can't go."

Then the phone rang. On the other end of the line was Don Cherry, the coach of the Rockies, and when I hung up the phone I knew I was on my way to Denver.

If there was a bright spot in being traded to one of the worst teams in hockey, it was playing for the man they call Grapes. No doubt, he was the coach I most enjoyed playing for. And from the moment I was traded, he did everything he could for my family and me. He told me I would be allowed to commute to Toronto between games to be with Ardell, who was two weeks away from giving birth. I quickly became the only player in the NHL playing only road games. In a matter of days, the hectic experience of being traded grew even more hectic. To be honest, it was hell. Exhaustion was beginning to set in, and I don't think I've ever been so tired in my entire life. Part of my time was spent playing for the Rockies, but most of my time was spent either in airplanes or with my family. If we played a game in Denver, I'd catch a flight to Chicago after the game, get there about seven in the morning, and then catch a connecting flight to Toronto where I'd get in about 9 a.m. All this time, the only sleep I got was on planes. The funny thing was that I might have been playing the best hockey I played that season, probably because I was so thankful for what Grapes was doing for me.

The fact that I was playing, but wasn't really part of the team, wasn't easy for Grapes or for the team. But Grapes had called a team meeting right after the trade and said,"This is the way it's going to be. We're going to accept it and go from there." The players accepted it, and I've always been thankful to Grapes for what he did for me. Hockey may be great, but it's not number one. Family is. Our beautiful daughter, Leah Bevin, was born on January fifteenth, and I was beside Ardell, acting as cheerleader all the way.

Playing for the Colorado Rockies could have been a horrible experience, except Don Cherry made sure it wasn't. After leaving Punch Imlach and the Toronto turmoil behind, Grapes make hockey fun again. All he asked of you was to give your best. If that's what you gave, and it wasn't good enough, "The other team must have been better," he'd say. Coaching the Rockies wasn't easy for him, considering he had just come from Boston where he coached the Bruins to the Stanley Cup finals. We weren't going to the Stanley Cup finals. Heck, we weren't even battling for a playoff spot.

Grapes may not have been the best technical coach in the world, but he was a tremendous motivator. He would say little things about pride and love for the game that would give you that extra boost to keep going. He'd throw in things all the time that made the game much more enjoyable. One game that always sticks in my mind was a night we were playing the Islanders in New York. With a minute and a half to go in the game, losing 4–1, Grapes called time out. I was on the ice with Randy Pierce, a pesky forward, and we skated toward the bench. Randy joked, "Well, Grapes, what do you want us to do? Tie it, or win it?"

He just looked out at the ice and said, "Boys, see that team over there? They're nine or ten goals better than us, but we've held them to a 4–1 score. I just want you to know one thing. Drinks are on me after the game."

After the game, he took us all for Chinese food.

That kind of summed up what Don Cherry was like. He knew how to keep enthusiasm in the game, even if we were losing night after night. The funny thing was, after all the travel, and having my family in one city with me in another, I was playing well for the Rockies. The year I was traded, I had 15 goals in 35 games for the Leafs, then went on to score 25 in 45 games for Colorado. I'll never forget a comment from Mike Bossy toward the end of that season. It was just after a game against the Islanders; the Rockies were headed for the golf course, and Mike was destined for another Cup.

"Lanny," Bossy said, "I just have to tell you something. Scoring 35 goals for the Colorado Rockies is like scoring 50 goals anywhere else."

Coming from Mike Bossy, the best goal scorer of his day, that really meant something to me. You remember things like that. Those were the type of comments that kept me going and helped keep things in perspective. To this day I'm thankful to Bossy for his words.

I didn't know it at the time, but when Grapes had gone out of his way to allow me the freedom to play, but not practice, with the Rockies, he was acting against the wishes of the general manager, Ray Miron. And for all I know, the owner of the Rockies, Arthur Imperatore, wasn't too pleased about it either.

Eventually, one thing became obvious to the players. A power struggle between Grapes and Miron had developed, and it was difficult to tell who was winning. Miron didn't agree with the preferential treatment I was receiving, but more than that, he was angry because it was Grapes, and not him, calling the shots. That was just one of the problems between them and one of the reasons that Grapes eventually lost the battle. Grapes thought his team was everything; Imperatore saw it only as a business.

If I were to put together a comparison chart of general managers, I'm not sure Ray Miron would even be on it. Certainly when compared to Jim Gregory and Cliff Fletcher he wouldn't make the grade. And to me, if a guy doesn't meet those standards, he doesn't fit in. Punch Imlach was a bothersome GM. Miron mostly wasn't anything. He had no presence in the club; no one knew when he was around. There wasn't the respect that a GM needs.

Ray's major problem was that he had no control. With Imperatore based in the East, Miron didn't know how to take command of a situation. He was trying, but he wasn't given the authority. We had no direction, and we got little respect. There wasn't any light at the end of the tunnel. We weren't making any strides forward. We were caught in hockey's no-man's land.

No one knew who we were, and no one cared.

No matter who else you played for, you got used to being treated in a first-class manner. Luxury hotels, great restaurants, top flight buses. The works. Not so with the Rockies. On most days you didn't know what to expect. Once, on Long Island, our team bus didn't arrive after a morning practice, and cabs were nowhere to be found. The players ended up on the highway outside the Nassau Coliseum, hitch-hiking back to the hotel.

Another night, in Chicago, we were waiting for our bus to take us to a game against the Blackhawks. We checked the parking lot, but there was only a banged-up old school van sitting there. We thought nothing of it and waited for a team bus to arrive. It was starting to get late, and we figured maybe we should take taxis to the game. All of a sudden, the driver from the banged-up school bus came over to us: "You guys aren't the Colorado Rockies, are you?" That's the way we travelled.

Grapes liked everybody in varying degrees, but he really loved his dog, Blue. Blue even had his own spot right inside the dressing room door, and everyone knew to tread carefully when passing Blue's "throne." One morning, a Hartford reporter rushed into the dressing room to get his story. He was in too much of a hurry for Blue's liking, and the dog grabbed the reporter's pant leg and hung on like any good guard dog! We were all yelling for Grapes to come and rescue the poor guy, but when Grapes came in, he surveyed the situation and bellowed, pointing to Blue, "That's the way I want you guys to play tonight!" He let that point sink in and then said, "OK, Blue, let the guy go." The reporter didn't stick around for his story!

Thank goodness we had guys on our team with a sense of humour. Walt McKechnie, who by that time was playing his twelfth season and for his eighth team, made life easier. "It could be worse," he'd say with a laugh. But we wondered how.

Walter's initiation with the Rockies happened one fateful night in Philadelphia. Wanting to get him into the game quickly, Grapes put Walt on the starting lineup with Paul Gagne and me as his wingers. Eleven seconds into the game it was 1-0 Flyers. Forty seconds later it was 2-0. As Walter slumped on the bench, Grapes went over and with a reassuring pat on the shoulder said, "McKech, welcome to Rocky Hockey!"

But just to show there were some bright spots with the team, after falling behind 4-1, the Rockies came back and tied those big, bad Flyers, with Walter assisting on the tying goal.

Bobby Schmautz was another guy who made life enjoyable on the Rockies. He was nearing the end of his career, playing for his fifth team, and was one of Grapes' favourite players. I thought he was an inspiration to us, the way he went out every night and played hard, at age thirty-six, as if it were the Stanley Cup finals. Schmautzie was truly one of the bright spots about playing for the Rockies. He was a lift of energy who gave everyone more heart because of what he demanded of others and of himself. He was also one of those guys who, wherever he went, was determined to have a few laughs. And believe me, we needed the laughs.

Hockey players are notorious for playing tricks in airports. There's the one where a player attaches a thread to a dollar bill and slides the bill around the airport floor, watching people try to pick it up. Gags like that break the monotony of travel. They're fun and they're harmless. Usually.

Schmautzie and I had a game we used to play in airports occasionally. The funniest time was in Edmonton, when we were waiting in line to clear customs. The gag works this way: Schmautzie would have a carry-on bag sitting by him, and he'd kick it. When he kicked it, I'd make the whining sound of a beaten dog, and no one could see me do it because of my moustache. Then he'd kick the bag again, and I'd yelp! Well, we started doing this in Edmonton, and everyone is staring at Schmautz. Grapes was in the corner laughing so hard he was crying. A lady moved towards Schmautzie and started furiously hitting him with her handbag. The customs officers, hearing all the commotion, arrived on the scene to check out what was going on. The woman was just out of control. So was the team—with laughter. She called us every name in the book. And when she found out there wasn't a dog in the bag, she was both angry and embarrassed.

Hockey aside, I was starting to love Denver. Sure, it was a tough first year, but guys like Grapes and Walter and Schmautzie made it easier, and so did Joel Quenneville, who was traded with me to Colorado. When you're traded with another player, a bond develops. Going into an unkown situation makes you look to each other for support. With Ardell and the girls in Toronto, Joel and I lived together, first in a hotel, later in a house we rented. He kept me young. I kept him on the straight and narrow. In time, Joel became like one of the family. At a crucial point in my life, Joel came to my rescue, though he may not have known it. I'll always be grateful for his laughter, his carefree ways and, more than anything, his friendship.

For all that was going wrong with the Rockies, there was something nice about playing in Denver. You could go anywhere in the city and nobody knew you and nobody cared. It was like a period of rejuvenation after the atmosphere in Toronto. Once my family moved to Denver, playing for the Rockies was fabulous!

When you're growing up you want to be the best. You want to reach a point where people recognize you for what you've achieved, what you've accomplished. In Toronto though, it had reached the point where it was difficult to go anywhere. My family's private moments often had to take a back seat to a well-meaning public. No matter what the team did in Denver, we took a back seat to the football Broncos and the basketball Nuggets. No matter what the Rockies did, we were destined for anonymity.

In plain English, the biggest problem with the Rockies was talent— we just didn't have enough. We had some older guys like Rene Robert, Schmautzie and McKech, who had played their best hockey elsewhere; some character guys in Ron Delorme and Mike Kitchen; and some young talented guys like Rob Ramage and Lucien Deblois. The one thing we didn't have was a goaltender. I guess I should rephrase that: We had goaltenders. We just didn't have any who helped us.

We went through goaltenders, it seemed, the way some teams go through towels. Grapes was hard on goaltenders, and I thought it was probably because he had come from Boston, where the Bruins were always strong in net. In Boston, they prided themselves in goals-against average. Hell, we were just trying to keep it under six a game. We went through five goaltenders in half a season. Ken Dryden would have had difficulty playing goal for the Colorado Rockies!

As the first season wound down, the players were starting to think that Grapes was winning the inner battle with Ray Miron. Most of us thought Grapes was going to wind up as general manager. We knew it was coming down to a power struggle, and because of what he meant to Denver and to hockey in Denver, we thought he would wind up on top. The one thing he had against him was that the club's ownership wasn't in Denver to see what he was doing. They were based in New Jersey, and what they didn't see was how Grapes sold hockey. He was an entertainer. He brought in the crowds. Of all the problems the Rockies had, Grapes wasn't one of them. And when he was let go, after the season ended, we were all disappointed.

If I learned anything from my father, it was honesty. He always told me to call a spade a spade, and I think I've done that. So, when Grapes got fired after what he had done for me, I had no choice but to speak out.

I said it was a mistake, the worst thing they could do. I said he wasn't the problem. Grapes had given me a chance to play for him, yet he also allowed me to be with my family at a time when that was very important to me. I knew how much he meant to hockey in Denver, and I was angry about what happened to him. I said so on television, on radio and in the papers.

Grapes was gone. The Rockies were in their usual shambles, and I had one odd thought: We were the worst team in the league, yet I didn't want to leave. We had things to prove.

9

ROCKY MOUNTAIN LOW

You can take the boy away from the Leafs, but you can't take the Leafs away from the boy. That's about how I felt in Colorado, playing for the struggling Rockies. Whenever I picked up a newspaper, I always checked the Maple Leafs' summaries first. I wanted to know who was doing what, what was going on. That's how my first half-season with the Rockies went. I knew how the Rockies were doing, so there wasn't much point in checking those stats. I was playing in Colorado, but my heart was in Toronto.

As I was about to report to my first training camp with the Rockies, a story broke in Toronto. The *Globe and Mail* headline of September 10, 1980, blared across

the sports page: "Ballard wants Lanny back on Leafs."
At first glance, it was the type of story that was easy to
ignore. For one thing, Harold Ballard liked to say
things. Anything. It didn't matter what, as long as his
name got in the paper! But this story was a little different; Imlach had suffered a heart attack three weeks
earlier, and Harold had taken over Punch's respon-
sibilities as general manager.

The *Globe* story, written by Bill Houston, said that
Harold was willing to send two or three players to the
Rockies to get me back. "I think we can reach an
agreement," Harold was quoted as saying.

At first, I was excited at the prospect of returning to
Toronto. We still had our home in Mississauga, so it
would have been easy to move back. But after a few
seconds of dreaming—you are allowed to dream—the
reality of the situation sunk in. I didn't really think a
trade to Toronto would ever materialize. It was just
another speculative story going nowhere. Deep down in
my heart, as much as I wanted it to happen, I knew it
wouldn't.

Maybe, in his own way, Harold was letting me know
that someone may have made a mistake. With Punch
out of the way for the time being, it was Harold's way of
sending a message. A trade never did materialize, and I
didn't hear an awful lot about it after that.

With talk of the Leaf trade over, it was time to start
playing hockey again, which is what I think the
Colorado Rockies were supposed to be doing, although
you were never quite sure. Ray Miron had won the
power struggle with Grapes, and we had a new coach,
Billy MacMillan, a guy who had played for the Leafs
before I did and then went on to play in Atlanta and
Long Island. When he finished his playing career, he
became an Islanders' assistant coach under Al Arbour.
Hiring MacMillan was supposed to be the Rockies way
of progress: If you're trying to improve, why not steal

from the best team in hockey! The logic was right, but that didn't mean it would work.

It wasn't that he was a bad coach. MacMillan simply wasn't forceful enough. He wasn't strong enough to coach a team that needed the type of help we did, and the Rockies certainly weren't strong enough as a team to help a rookie coach. What hurt Billy the most was lack of experience. He cared, and he worked hard at the job, but... there was always a "but."

MacMillan was hired to get us going in the right direction. Under Grapes, we had won 19 games. With MacMillan coaching a slightly better club we won 22 games. So much for improvement. But the good news was we didn't finish in last place. The Winnipeg Jets did, with only nine wins.

I remember one night, in December 1980, the Winnipeg Jets were going for a record: most consecutive games without a win! It was a record no one wanted to hold, and the media were there in full force. *Sports Illustrated* even appeared to record the event, and who was the opponent on that historic night? The mighty Rockies. We stopped the Jets in their quest for glory, stole their *Sports Illustrated* story and wrote one more chapter for Rocky Hockey. The Colorado Rockies lost the game.

We struggled through most of the 1980-81 season with one of the same problems we had the year before—goaltending. But on February 26, we acquired Phil Myre, and his experience really helped. After all, when you're playing goal for the Rockies and win 6, lose 5 and tie 4, you're ready for the Vezina Trophy.

In March, another trade brought Glenn Resch and Steve Tambellini in exchange for Mike McEwan. As happy as I was to have them as teammates, I felt sorry for Chico and Tambi when they were dealt to the Rockies from the Stanley Cup Champion Islanders just minutes before the NHL trade deadline that season.

Talk about culture shock! They were going from the best team in the league to a team that was almost the worst; from filet to hamburger! We were in Washington, heading to New York to play the Rangers, when we heard about the trade. It sounded too good to be true!

We won our first game with Chico in the net, and Steve scored the winning goal. It looked to me like we made the greatest trade in the history of the league. Especially when you consider that Mike McEwan, the oddest of the Rockies' players, was heading in the other direction. McEvan wasn't just different from the usual hockey player, he was different from the rest of the world.

The March trade added two great guys, even if they weren't exactly thrilled to be there. After the excitement of our first victory with Chico and Steve, it didn't take long for that old reality to set in again: Chico wasn't a magician and Tambi, though a gifted centre, couldn't score 80 goals a season. Even with them in our lineup, we didn't have enough time to make a playoff run, nor did we have enough talent. The Rockies continued to flounder the last two weeks of that season until it mercifully ended, and we all looked forward to the fall because we knew it couldn't get any worse.

The team continued to make moves, even if they didn't always make sense. Miron retired or was pushed out, it was difficult to tell which. As a player, I was hoping that some miracle-worker would come out of the woodwork, take over the Rockies and establish pro hockey in Denver. Everyone was surprised when Billy MacMillan was named general manager of the club. Here was a guy who had only coached in the league for one year, and suddenly he was being made GM. Billy named Bert Marshall, another ex-Islander, as the club's coach. I was starting to figure this whole thing out: We were the New York Islander's farm team!

As a general manager, MacMillan was very aggressive.

He knew the Rockies were in trouble and he was doing his best to save them. Before the 81–82 season had even begun, the Rockies seemed like a different team, at least on paper. For starters, we would have Chico in goal for a whole season and Tambi at centre. MacMillan had also gone shopping and spent a bundle, reported at more than $1 million, for the release and signing of five Europeans.

When I heard that the Rockies had signed five Europeans, I remembered the Maple Leafs and the impact Borje Salming and Inge Hammarstrom had made on the NHL. We've turned the corner, I thought. But when training camp began, it didn't take us long to realize those five players weren't the answer to our hockey problems. If anything, they were going to push us one step closer to folding. Three of the five wound up on our Fort Worth farm team. Not only were they not good enough to play for us, they weren't good enough to play in Fort Worth, and none of them really cared. They put in their time, collected their paycheques and spent the rest of the time aggravating those of us who were trying. On our first trip into Los Angeles that year, instead of spending the day of the game preparing, they rented a big white limousine and toured Beverley Hills. That was our big financial deal: We signed tourists!

Billy seemed to be into making deals; we were lucky to get a guy like Dwight Foster who really added a spark of enthusiasm and a whole lot of heart. We were lucky to get guys like Bob Lorimer and Dave Cameron, who put a Band-Aid on our situation but weren't the blood transfusion that we so desperately needed. Unfortunately, we had mortgaged the Rockies' future, but the house we were building wasn't a dream home, it was more like the *House on Elm Street.*

Billy MacMillan made lots of off-season moves but gained little. So what did he do early in the season, when the team looked little better than it did the year before? He replaced Bert Marshall as coach with Marshall Johnston.

Just into my third season with the Rockies, Marshall Johnston became my fourth head coach. That summed up the Colorado Rockies' existence more than anything else. I played 142 games for the Rockies and four different people coached the team. Constant change, no improvement. That seemed to be the Rockies style. It wasn't a stable franchise or a stable environment, and it was hard to get consistency out of the players or the fans.

The people I really felt sorry for were the kids: Brent Ashton, Paul Gagne, Joe Cirella, Aaron Broten, Rob Ramage, Joel Quenneville and Steve Tambellini. It was an impossible situation for those young men. No one was giving them any direction. They had dreamed about playing in the NHL, and they had been disillusioned. If the team had had better direction, perhaps the franchise would still be in Denver today. The problem with playing in Denver was that no one would wait for tomorrow.

Not only did we have a new general manager and two new coaches, but we had a new owner as well. Arthur Imperatore, who owned the Rockies from New Jersey, had sold the club to Peter Gilbert, a cable television magnate, who owned the club from Buffalo. Just what we needed, more absentee ownership.

Nearing the end of a road trip, we lost 9-2 in Calgary against the Flames. I should have suspected something was up. I had played the first 13 games of the year and then wound up with a separated shoulder. I missed only five games, and I've never felt such pressure to get back in the lineup as I did then. Everyone from coaches to management was making sure I was ready to play. It was as if I were quietly being pushed. After the game at the Corral, I walked out of the building with my mom and dad and we saw Al MacNeil, the coach for the

Flames, with his assistant, Pierre Page. "Keep your chin up," MacNeil said to me. "Things will get brighter." I don't know if he meant anything by that, although I suspect he did.

The next morning, we boarded the plane for Winnipeg and Billy MacMillan was nowhere to be found; we just thought he was embarrassed to travel with the Colorado Rockies. After the plane landed, I saw an Air Canada agent hand Marshall Johnston a note. As I was walking towards the terminal, he called me aside.

"Lanny," he said, "you're going back to Calgary."

My first thought was that something had happened, that someone was sick.

"What is it? What's wrong?" I said.

The possibility of a trade had never even dawned on me.

"I'm traded?" I shouted at him. I couldn't believe they had traded me. I was mad. In the middle of an airport, I was yelling at Marshall Johnston.

"I can't believe you traded me," I yelled. In retrospect, I can't believe how angry I was. All I could think about was rejection. The worst team in the NHL didn't want me! Think about that for a minute. It hurts. I stood in the airport in shock. It was as if time stood still. Getting traded once was enough. You think it can't happen again.

By this time, the players had all boarded the team bus. I wanted a chance to talk to them; I was concerned for those guys. We had been through a lot together. When you're on a losing hockey team that doesn't have a hope in hell of going anywhere and you're a long way from home, the guys in the dressing room become family, the best friends you've got. I said to Marshall, "I'm going on the bus to talk to the guys for a minute." I told him to stay off. I don't know what I would have done if he had said no.

I explained to the guys that I had been traded. By

then, they knew what was going on. I tried to tell them what a super bunch of guys they were, but how do you tell Tambi, the Pizza Man, what a great friend he'd been and how much it meant when he waited for me as Marshall Johnston told me the news? How do you tell guys like Tambellini and Foster that they made life in Denver fun instead of just being part of a losing hockey club? How do you tell Chico that you'd miss those late night discussions, that his insight was next to none? How do you tell Rob Ramage and Brent Ashton that their time to shine was coming? How do you tell guys like Mike Kitchen and Ron Delorme that their determination was an inspiration to us all? I shook everybody's hand and wished them luck, then left the bus in tears, both disillusioned and disappointed. It hurt inside. I walked away from the Rockies for the last time and went to phone Ardell to tell her we'd be moving again.

After a trade, after a hurt like that, the one thing you want is someone close to talk to. There isn't a more lonely feeling in the world than being in a strange city with no one around. It was frightening to be alone at the Winnipeg Airport. I watched the team bus pull away... without me. Suddenly I remembered that my equipment was on that bus. Rocky Hockey had done it to me one last time.

10

COMING HOME

On the plane ride back to Calgary, I started to work it all over in my mind. Lanny McDonald and a draft pick for Bob MacMillan and Don Lever. Who won the deal? I was hoping the draft pick would turn out to be a good one. (Bill Claviter, where are you?)

I think the pressure is what I feared most about coming home and playing in front of friends and family. It wasn't like the pressure in Toronto. I had already made it; now I had to prove I still had it.

It was funny arriving back in Calgary that night; Frank, my father-in-law, had taken me to the airport in the morning as a member of the Colorado Rockies. Nine hours later he picked me up at the same airport as the newest member of the Calgary Flames.

Once you get over the initial shock of the situation and try to figure out what's in store for you, you start to settle down. I had been following the Flames that season because they were struggling and we were in the same division. They were the team the Rockies kept cheering against. But I also knew they were a club that had some talent. I had been in Alberta the year before, their first season in Calgary, and watched them advance to the Stanley Cup semifinals. I knew they were a better team than their record showed, and I knew that with players like Kent Nilsson, Guy Chouinard and Mel Bridgman, there'd be no shortage of good centres to play with.

Everything had been nice and quiet in Toronto—as nice and quiet as Toronto ever gets—until Punch took over the Leafs. Then I found myself right in the middle of all the action that was happening off the ice. From there, I went to Denver; and when you played for the Colorado Rockies you played with a cloud over your head, not knowing if the franchise was living, dying or merely changing addresses.

With my trade to Calgary, I was willing to greet stability with open arms. I thought I was walking into a calm, quiet situation. It was only the Flames' second season in Calgary, and if the team were moving anywhere, it was up in the standings. Ownership was established. Cliff Fletcher was a top-notch general manager. Everything was stable. At least, that's what I thought as I joined the club in November of 1981, sore shoulder and all.

Still, it wasn't easy. I remember the first morning going to the Stampede Corral, the old home of the Flames. I couldn't wait to get into the dressing room. Even though Al Coates, who was then the public relations director for the team, did everything he could to make me feel welcome immediately, I didn't want to walk into a room full of strangers. I wanted to be the first guy in. I did know Bearcat Murray, who had been my trainer during the short stint I had with the Calgary Centennials. Bearcat and I had seen each other over the years, and it was nice to know I'd have at least one old friend around. He had two sweaters ready for me, seven or nine, whichever I preferred. I said I'd take nine: That blue-and-white seven had been a long time ago!

The only players I really knew were Phil Russell—he and I had battled each other since our junior days— and Bob Murdoch, who I knew from Players' Association meetings.

I also knew Mel Bridgman, mainly from the Leafs-Flyers wars. I must admit that the way I got to know Mel wasn't the way I would suggest getting to know him; I remember fighting Mel three times in a single game. At the end of a period, a brawl started between Jack Valiquette of the Leafs and Moose Dupont of Philadelphia. I stepped in to help Jack, and out of nowhere, Mel came charging in, and we fought. After the fight, Darryl turned to me and said, "Well, you lost that one. You're going to have to fight him again." Later, when a linesman had gone to break up another altercation, Mel and I were standing there eyeing each other, and we started again. It seemed like the thing to do. When they broke us apart, Darryl commented, "That one was a standoff, I think you can take him the next time." We went for a third round. Afterwards, Darryl told me, "You're batting .500, Mac. I think you won the last one."

"You don't fight bad," I said to Mel, exhausted as only a hockey fight can make you.

"You fight pretty good yourself; you must be a Westerner," Mel said.

Mel and I laughed about that incident when we became teammates. It felt good to be able to reminisce with someone and chuckle over events of years past. I still think that the difficult process of being traded is easier if you're traded *with* someone.

When I arrived in Calgary, the team wasn't exactly on a roll, and I felt the pressure for a variety of reasons. It wasn't easy stepping in and trying to replace two popular guys. The human aspect is sometimes the hardest part of being traded; both Bob MacMillan and Don Lever were popular players in the dressing room, on the ice and with the fans. They were well-liked among the players, and everyone on the team thought of them as friends. It wasn't that I felt resentment from anyone for taking their place, but I think a lot of players were taking a wait-and-see attitude about accepting me. Without being aware of it, they were putting extra pressure on me and I was already putting enough on myself.

A lot was expected of the Flames that season, and, as usual, I expected a lot of myself. The Flames had advanced to the semifinals during their first season in Calgary, knocking off the Philadelphia Flyers in the process. Suddenly, in their second season, nothing was going right. I attribute some of their first-year success to the trade factor. When a player is traded, he does his utmost to play his best and make an impression. But when an entire team trades cities the way the Flames did, all the players make an effort to play well, and it's a fresh start for the whole club. Collectively, they have something to prove, and in that first year the Flames proved to be a very good hockey team.

But that was the first year. The second year is another story entirely. The team had problems, of that there was no doubt. But I had a few problems of my own. I had badly separated my shoulder in Colorado, and when I rushed back early to play, I wasn't ready. I needed time to heal. But when you get traded to a new club, you really don't want to ask for a week off, whatever the reason. It just doesn't work that way. So there I was, trying to nurse a bum shoulder and perform well in spite of the condition I was in.

I was still in a state of transition, but it was good to be in a stable environment once again. I had become tired of wondering if the Rockies were going to survive in Denver. I'd seen owners like Arthur Imperatore and Peter Gilbert, who owned the club from several thousand miles away and believed that ownership was a business deal only and didn't require personal involvement. I had also seen Harold Ballard, who was an integral part of the daily life of his team.

Having been exposed to such diverse attitudes, coming to Calgary was like a breath of fresh mountain air. It was a real pleasure to be involved with six of the finest individuals I've ever met: Harley Hotchkiss, Doc and B.J. Seaman, Norman Green, Normie Kwong and Ralph Scurfield, the owners of the Flames. These people really care about the hockey club, the community and the relationship between club and community. They have a hands-off policy when it comes to running the team, something that is rare today in pro sports. They let the hockey club be run the way it should be run.

Each of the owners has gone out of his way to make the Flames and their families feel like part of the club. Their friendly manner and supportive attitude has helped make a successful franchise. Win or lose, they're in the dressing room after the game, always encouraging the guys. They keep a low profile, but they want to win as much as Harold Ballard does. They just go about their business in a different way.

My first game as a Flame was against the Los Angeles Kings, and I must admit I was nervous. Although I didn't score in my debut, I couldn't remember the last time I had played a game where I enjoyed myself so much. The Flames won with ease, and I think the nicest part of that game was the fact that we weren't trailing early. We crushed the Kings 7–1, and it was more fun than I'd had in years! It took me a lot longer to score my first goal as a Calgary Flame than I would have liked—

seven games that seemed like a season—and I think the fans were as relieved as I was when the puck finally went in the net. It was a shorthanded goal against the New York Islanders, and the piano was finally off my back!

There was a lot of talk then about the Atlanta connection. Most of the Flames players had played in Atlanta before the franchise was moved to Calgary. Most of them loved Atlanta, but there they were known as a good team that never lived up to people's expectations. People blamed it on the climate or the fact that they weren't in a hockey environment. Those excuses ended when the team moved to Calgary, but management felt that some of the lingering attitudes prevailed.

At the time, the media was reporting that the Flames' players were doing their best to get coach Al MacNeil fired, but I don't know if that was entirely true. What I do know is that the Flames' players weren't happy about anything: Calgary, MacNeil, housing prices, not being in Atlanta, hockey, everything.

There was a certain uneasiness on the team because we weren't winning, and I kept reading in the papers about the internal problems of the club. But at that point, I had worries of my own: getting healthy, performing well and adjusting to a new city. I was too new with the Flames to be involved in something old.

As the year continued, the complaining continued. Losing breeds dissatisfaction. We were always having players' meetings; we had meetings to figure out when the next meeting would be. It just gave players a chance to get things off their chests. I think we had more meetings than wins that season.

The club didn't really improve much as the season went on. We played well at times, but not enough times to make a difference. At the end of that year, Al was replaced as coach, and the move to assistant general manager was probably the best thing that ever happened to him. Away from the pressure of coaching, he's enjoying hockey now, the way someone who has put his life into the game deserves to enjoy it. A further dismantling of the old Atlanta nucleus took place. Bill Clement retired and has gone on to star as the colour commentator for ESPN hockey telecasts. Willi Plett was traded to the Minnesota North Stars, Pat Riggin and Ken Houston went to Washington.

When I was first traded to the Flames, I figured I'd wind up playing on a line centred by Guy Chouinard, Mel Bridgman or Kent Nilsson. To a winger, the centreman is always the key to your line. The one centre I didn't expect to be playing with was Jim Peplinski, but that's exactly where I wound up, with Jamie Hislop on the left wing. While Peplinski and Hislop were both hard workers, neither had been known for their scoring abilities.

Maybe because no one expected it, we clicked as a line. We snuck up on teams. Toward the end of the season, my shoulder had healed, and I was back on a roll. Our line was hot, and I was getting that special feeling again. It's difficult to explain, really, but as an athlete, you know when it's there and you know when it's not. Generally, we call it confidence, but it's something much greater than that. It's stepping on the ice and knowing that things are going right for you. It's shooting without looking, knowing you're going to score. It's feeling good about the game, about yourself, about everything. After a rocky start with the Flames, I was starting to feel that everything was going my way. I wound up scoring 34 goals in 55 games for the Flames, which is just a notch below the 50-goal pace. I finished the season with 40 goals, having scored six with the Rockies. With everything falling into place, I felt a certain amount of confidence heading into the playoffs, even if we didn't finish exactly where we wanted to be.

Through most of the season, we had been in a neck-

and-neck race with the Vancouver Canucks for home-ice advantage in the Smythe Division standings. Oddly enough, the night we blew second place we played the Rockies in Denver. It was the last home game for the Colorado Rockies. The team was eventually sold again and this time moved from Denver to New Jersey, where they became the Devils. In the dying seconds of that final game, I realized how sad it was to see Denver lose a team that had a good base of fan support. The fans had stood by the Rockies through five lean seasons and were there cheering madly that last game, even though they suspected the team would be moving.

Well, we lost a game we had to win. And it cost us second place. In the long run, it might have cost us a lot more. Vancouver finished second, swept us out of the playoffs in three straight games, and because of a series of unlikely circumstances, played the New York Islanders for the Stanley Cup. We thought we had a better team than Vancouver, but the Canucks were in the finals and we were at home watching. I felt a little sick about it but saw it as a sign that we had to be more prepared for next season.

Our battle with Vancouver was closer than losing three straight would indicate. But they found ways to win, and, considering Roger Neilson was coaching, their strategies were really no surprise. One of the many ploys Neilson used was to have Tiger Williams shadow me. I must admit, it worked. I didn't score a goal in the series.

It was during those playoffs that a Tiger Williams-Lanny McDonald feud was first labelled in the media. Tiger, Darryl and I were linemates on the Leafs, and there was a friendship then. But that was a long time ago, and things have changed.

The Tiger I knew in Toronto is not the same one who openly admitted to trying to break my ankle in that Vancouver series. My respect for Tiger as a hockey

Growing up. At 21 months of age; at 6; and at age 8, with my dad, Lorne, and my brother Lynn, 12, beside him.

The best line in junior hockey; Tommy Lysiak (R),
Boyd Anderson (C) and me.
Photo by Morely Fach, Medicine Hat.

Celebrating a 1967 championship with the Hanna
Bantam Elks.
Photo by Hunts' Photography, Calgary.

You've got to keep your head up when Larry Robinson is behind you.
Photo by Robert Shaver.

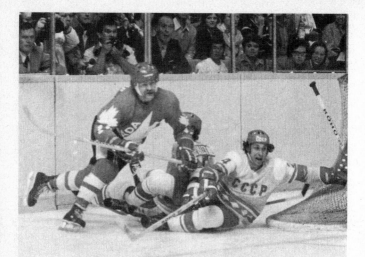

On top of the world. Beating the Soviets in the 1976
Canada Cup tournament.

Not a bad line to start with in the 1983 all-star game.
Wayne Gretzky, Al Secord and me.
Photo by Jimmy Lippa.

Great moments. Paul Baxter catches me after I scored an overtime goal against the Oilers, forcing a seventh game in 1984 Stanley Cup playoffs.
Photo by Pat Price Pic/Canada Wide.

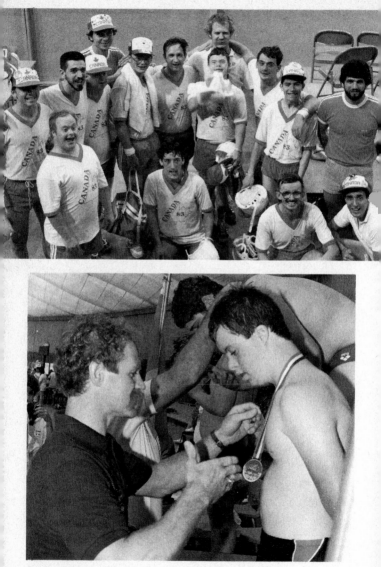

Special times with special friends— with Special
Olympians at 1986 National Games in Calgary.
Photo by Brad Watson.

My favourite picture! Me and Ardell.
Photo by Candy Oliver.

A day in the life. B.J. on my shoulders. Andra heading
for a cartwheel. Leah running and Ardell looking on.
Photo by Bruce Stotesbury.

Time out to welcome the newest rookie.
Photo by Michael Drew, Sun.

player diminished when he said that. There's a big difference between playing aggressively to win a game and playing the way he sometimes does now. I've never really figured him out, and to be honest, I'm not even going to try. The one thing I do know is that Tiger still works extremely hard with the Special Olympics, and that reminds me of the Tiger I once knew.

When a season ends as quickly as ours did, against the Canucks, it gives you a lot of time for reflection. Despite the turmoil and the abrupt ending of the season, I was happy to be in Calgary, and I felt good about myself again, about hockey and about the city that was my new home. Normally you have to wait for a season to end, for all the cards to be played before you can put things into perspective, and it was that way with me after my first season with the Flames. As I look back now, I see one thing: That trade to the Flames was one of the best things that has happened to me, especially after being in Denver for parts of three seasons.

The years in Denver were like a holiday of sorts, away from media attention, away from the mainstream of hockey. It was a time when I realized how fleeting fame is. You realize then you're only human and you're only doing a job, different than most jobs, but no more important than any other. Being in Denver gave me time to put life into proper perspective, to realize that the world didn't revolve around hockey. In Denver I learned a lot that prepared me for and enhanced my move to Calgary.

In Denver I was a nobody in the sports world, another hockey player for a team no one knew or cared about. Calgary put me back in the mainstream of hockey, and it would have been easy to get caught up in the media hype of "Lanny's homecoming." That's where family helps; they made me remember that I am husband, father, brother-in-law, friend, son, neighbour and then hockey player. Their guidance and support helped me realize that it's much more important to be Lanny the person than Lanny the hockey player.

If there is any benefit to being traded other than the career aspects, it's the friends you make. One of the first people I became friendly with in Calgary was Jim Peplinski.

Pepper and I have something in common: We're both practical jokers. Each NHL team has its share of pranksters, and as inane as it appears from the outside, the crazy jokes and tricks are a good break from the daily routine of a long season. The problem was, Pepper was getting the better of me!

Pepper had become famous for scaring me, and my nerves were on edge. I always used to tell him that he had to get up pretty early in the morning to outsmart "The Fox." It sounded good, even if it didn't always work that way. I made an arrangement with Kevin LaVallee, Pep's roommate: I would get the key to their room, sneak up to the room and surprise Pepper the same way he'd been scaring me. What I didn't know was that Kevin was a double agent; he led me to believe Pepper didn't know about my plans.

Quietly, I snuck up to the hotel room, opened the door, found a dark closet and prepared to get back at Pepper. As I was going into the closet to hide, something lunged out of the closet at me. It was dark, I couldn't see and I was scared spitless! I fell backwards, right into the hall and halfway into the bathroom. I didn't know if the guy from the closet had a knife or a gun or whatever. I'm sure Pepper has never laughed so hard.

Later on during that same road trip, Pepper fell asleep on the airplane. Once he was snoring, I stole one of his cowboy boots and gave it to one of the guys a few rows behind him. Somehow, the boot disappeared. Pep thought I had it. I didn't know who had it. So when we got to Calgary, there's poor old Pep, hobbling through the terminal with one boot on and one foot in a white sock. Pepper called the airport later to see if they had found his boot, and, not knowing he had called, I did the same. Both of us went to rescue the boot, but I beat him to it. When he arrived at the airport, it was nowhere to be found, and he figured his boot was gone forever. A few weeks later, on another airplane, we were being served dinner. While most of us had steak, Jim Peplinski's dinner looked an awful lot like a cowboy boot!

It was instances like this and guys like Pep that made my first year in Calgary so enjoyable. As I look back on that season, it was summed up by what happened in my first game as a Calgary Flame. I stepped onto the ice for my first shift, and I heard a lot of noise. At first, I didn't know what it was all about, but when I looked around, I realized the fans were giving me a rousing ovation. They welcomed me to Calgary with open arms and made me realize I had been away too long.

Gosh, it was great to be home!

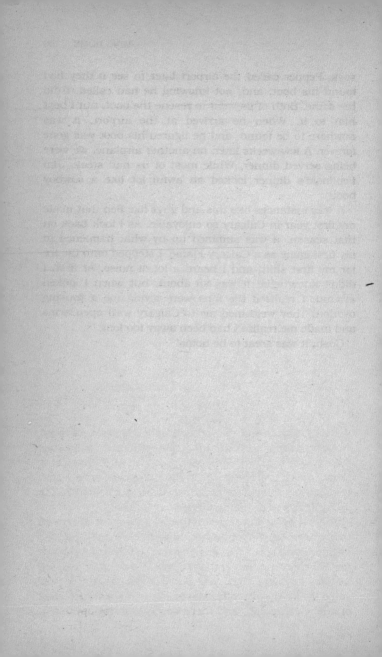

11

THE MIDAS TOUCH

Wayne Gretzky and Lanny McDonald. Me and Gretzky. Gretzky and me. No matter how it was put, no matter how it was said, I still liked the sound of it. And for a brief time in my career, the 1982–83 season to be exact, I found myself involved in a scoring race with the greatest scorer in the history of the game.

There's something about the beginning of a season that brings out the optimism in athletes. When the year begins, you feel like this is the one you're going to win the Stanley Cup. Except, of course, if you were playing for the Rockies. Then you felt like this was the year you'd make the playoffs. Maybe. But this was the start of a new campaign, and there was reason for optimism, despite the fact that the Flames were coming off a difficult season.

We had a new coach, new players, a new approach. It was like a fresh start for everybody, and because it was all so new, everything was exciting. Bob Johnson took over the Flames that season and became the ninth head coach I had played for in ten NHL seasons. The coach was new, his assistant—Bob Murdoch, who retired as a player to become a coach—was new. And a large portion of the team had been changed. As if the trading of Eric Vail, Bob MacMillan, Don Lever and Brad Marsh the season before hadn't been enough, Willi Plett, Pat Riggin, Ken Houston and Bill Clement had all been sent packing in the off season. The dismantling of the so-called Atlanta connection, eight players, all considered prominent, had taken place in the span of less than a season.

I was starting my first full season with the Flames, having settled in after the trade from Colorado. In the off-season, the Flames had acquired some well-known veteran players, including goaltender Don Edwards and centre Doug Risebrough. Everyone was ready to prove themselves again, including a twenty-nine-year-old veteran—me.

I have not always been the fastest of starters, but this year I'd had a good camp, one of those where everything seemed to be going my way, no matter who I played with. And I quickly learned that when you play for Bob Johnson, you play with everyone. We all wondered what it was going to be like, playing for a college coach, but his approach was so optimistic, so fresh, so different that I think we liked the change. There's always a transition period with a new coach, and some guys adapt better then others. I didn't need to adapt. The way things were going in camp, I was ready to start the season.

Johnson had put together what I thought was a

dream line when the season began in Edmonton: Guy Chouinard playing centre with Kent Nilsson at left wing and me on right wing. Chouinard had scored 50 goals in Atlanta, Nilsson had 49 two seasons back and I scored 40 the season before. The Million Dollar Line someone dubbed us, and that's how I felt playing beside the two most talented players I'd ever been with.

Well, the Million Dollar Line wasn't worth its billing. We lasted one night together in the NHL, when we allowed four goals against in a loss to Edmonton. We might have had a lot of offence on our line, but not much defence. We never did play together again, except on the power play, where I played the left side and Kent played the right.

The dream line may not have worked out, but everything else went my way early in the season, both on the ice and off. On October 18, 1982, Ardell gave birth to our first son, Barrett James. A beautiful nine-pound boy. Thank goodness he looked like his mother!

Babies have been good for my career. When Andra was born, I went on a scoring streak in Toronto. After Leah was born, I got hot in Colorado. And the same was true after Barrett was born. It seems every time one of our children is born, it's been a very exciting hockey year for me. I don't think that it's because the pressure is off or anything like that. Ardell and the children are the most important part of my life, and to see my little family grow makes me realize there's nothing quite like being a father.

After Barrett was born, the goals just kept going in. After 16 games, I had 16 goals to lead the league. Gretzky had 15. All of a sudden, everyone was talking about the Calgary-Edmonton rivalry and the race between the two goal scorers. It was an exciting time for me, especially after spending a couple of years in Colorado out of the mainstream of the hockey world. It was thrilling to be back in the centre of things.

It was a tremendous time, really. Every day I would check the paper to see what Gretzky had done. If he had scored the night before, I'd want to score that night. I was putting pressure on myself to keep up. That season I began to understand what Gretzky must go through year after year to produce the way he does. For me, it was just one of those years when everything went right. It didn't matter how much other teams checked, I was in such an emotional state and my confidence was so high I felt I could score no matter what they did.

To be able to play at the tempo Gretzky does, game after game, year after year, is phenomenal. The kind of pressure on him means he goes above and beyond the call of duty answering the bell. A lot of people don't realize how much he's meant to the game. I have nothing but admiration for him and the utmost respect.

You don't like Gretzky when you're playing for another team. But that doesn't mean you don't admire him. There's a difference between the two. You don't like him because usually he's the guy who's responsible for you losing. At the same time, you recognize the kind of rare ability and awesome talent he has.

The NHL all-star game that season was on Long Island, the home of the New York Islanders. Gretzky was voted to start for the Campbell Conference team at centre; Al Secord, the rugged winger from Chicago, started on left; and I was starting on right wing. By the time of the game, Gretzky had scored 46. In my last game before the all-star break, I scored three goals and went to the game leading the league with 47.

I played only one shift of that all-star game with Gretzky and Secord and wound up on a line with Marcel Dionne and Brian Sutter, two guys I have known for a long time. Before the game, the coaches gave their usual, "Let's-go-out-and-give-it-our-best-shot" speech— in other words, they said, "This is the all-star game, let's not get anybody hurt out there!"

Brian Sutter, the physical captain and inspirational leader of the St. Louis Blues, leaned over to me and said with a smile, "Hey Mac, you and I only know one way to play, and if we don't do that, we'll be in a lot of trouble." You see, we played hockey only one way out West— bump and grind! He was kidding, of course, but there was a message in what he was saying: "You may be having a career season as far as goal scoring is concerned, but you can't forget what got you there." I hadn't.

I scored a goal in the all-star game but couldn't keep pace with Gretzky that night. While it looked like goaltender John Garrett was on his way to win the most-valuable-player-of-the-game award, Gretzky took the car away from him. He scored four goals on Pelle Lindbergh, and, hard as I tried, I couldn't match him the rest of the season.

I finished that season with 66 goals, 19 more than I had ever scored before. Gretzky finished with 71.

When you've scored 47 goals in a season, you always hope that one year you'll score 50. But 66 was beyond my wildest dreams. That's the type of season it was for me. As Eric Duhatschek wrote in the *Calgary Herald*, I had the Midas touch: Everything I touched turned to goals! And my grandkids will be hearing about those 66 forever!

It's one thing to be successful. It's another to understand why. I always knew I could score, but averaging 40 goals a season and scoring more than 60 are two completely different things. Almost everything that was supposed to go right that season went right, and that included the man who happened to be my centre, Guy Chouinard.

Of the 66 goals I scored, Chouinard had the first assists on 31 of them, which is truly an incredible number. I point that out because it's important to me, knowing how much Guy contributed to my success. Chouinard was a magician. He was as uncanny a passer as anyone I've ever encountered. He could get you the puck when you were sure there wasn't a hope in hell of getting it through. Guy used to say, "Just keep your stick on the ice, Mac, and I'll put the puck on it." Once in a while, when he made one of those unbelievable passes, he'd say with a smile, "See, what did I tell you?"

Not a lot of people outside Calgary knew about Chouinard. It's a shame, really, considering his ability. He was able to make a cross-ice pass better than anyone I've ever seen. I've played with great players like Sittler and Lysiak, but I've never played with anyone who could do what Guy could do with a puck. I always thought I was best suited to playing with left-handed shooting centres, but Guy shot right and could pass better off his backhand than most players could on their forehand. We used to play a little game after practice every once in a while: A few of us would line up pucks on the blue line and shoot for the crossbar. The last guy to hit it had to buy lunch for the rest of us. Guy never had to buy lunch. Need I say more?

One of the differences that season was the power play. I played the opposite wing which gave me more of an angle for shooting. Bob Johnson insisted that his wingers play that way. We did that a little bit in Toronto under Roger Neilson, but with Johnson we did it all the time. Chouinard played the right point, Nilsson played the right side, and I was the guy they were trying to feed on the left wing.

The league was becoming speed conscious, and that may have been part of Guy's undoing. In his own humorous way, Guy always claimed that he skated faster against the tougher teams; he said that having someone chase you made you skate faster! Actually, I always thought he was a better skater than anyone gave him credit for. He looked slower than he actually was, but he had a way of getting where he had to be.

Guy never did get the credit he deserved for his part in my 66-goal season: He was traded before the next season began. But he made a large contribution to that peak year, and I hope he realizes it.

When I left Long Island after the all-star game, I had 47 goals, and I knew that 50 wouldn't be far away. Gretzky had scored 92 the previous season, devaluing the 50-goal mark in some people's minds, but certainly not in mine. I had always wanted to score 50 goals in the NHL, and I knew that this would be my season to do it. The question, of course, was when?

If you dream of scoring 50 goals, you also dream of how you're going to score that magic fiftieth. It's always a classic. An end-to-end rush. A perfect shot. A great passing play. A game winner in the dying seconds. The night I scored my fiftieth— against the Buffalo Sabres— it was the Flames' only goal in a 5-1 loss at the Memorial Auditorium. I felt like celebrating the goal but not the game.

It wasn't one of your classic goals. Phil Russell had kept the puck in at the blue line and taken a shot on net that Bob Sauve stopped. The rebound went to Eddy Beers, and after Sauve made a second save, I tucked the puck under him for the goal. It wasn't the way I dreamed of scoring my fiftieth but I wasn't about to give it back, either.

"Hey," Sauve yelled at me when the game ended.

"What?" I shouted back.

"Couldn't you have waited until tomorrow to do that?"

That night we bussed to Toronto after the game and the following night played the Leafs in Game 61 of the season. If I could have changed anything about my fiftieth goal, I guess I would have waited just one more day and scored it in Maple Leaf Gardens, where I made my start— in front of the fans who had treated me so well.

The response from around the league to my scoring

50 goals was incredible. The telegrams and good wishes I received were heart-warming. Just a few days before I scored, I turned thirty, and the *Sun* ran a page of poems written by Calgarians about me. Stuff like:

> Gentlemen, I propose a toast
> To a man who is giving his most.
> Happy Birthday to Lanny
> Your skills are uncanny.
> Without you, the Flames would roast!

As nice as something like that was, it was also kind of embarrassing. Hockey is a team sport, and to be singled out from the rest of the guys is difficult.

I didn't have time to dwell on my fiftieth goal. I had to play the next day. Normally, on the day of a game, I like to sleep in the afternoon, but the rest didn't come easy that day. I replayed the goal in my mind a million times. It had finally happened!

Back in Calgary, the Flames recognized my landmark goal with a special ceremony. Guy Chouinard, the only other Flame to have scored 50 goals and the man who set up so many of mine, presented me with a plaque that held the puck I scored the goal with. Two of my former coaches, Jack Shupe and Red Kelly, were flown in for the ceremony. Imagine how I felt, having these three men, who all played a large part in helping me to mould my career, be there to share my happiness.

I still take great pride in that plaque I received from Guy, and I also have pucks from my sixtieth goal on. Gary Taylor, who does the video work for the Flames, made a tape of my fiftieth, sixtieth and sixty-first to sixty-sixth goals, and it's also something I cherish. When times are bad or my confidence is lagging, I'll pull out that old tape and hope it brings some of that magic back.

For me, it turned out to be a regular season I'll never forget, even though the playoffs were somewhat anticlimactic. We beat the Vancouver Canucks in a very physical, punishing playoff series and then learned something from the Edmonton Oilers in a one-sided loss. We found out just how far we had to go to compete with the Oilers. Because I was injured, I only played seven of the nine playoff games, but even the playoff disappointment couldn't put a damper on the season.

The Bill Masterton Trophy is presented every season during the Stanley Cup Finals to the NHL player who best exemplifies the qualities of perseverance, sportsmanship and dedication to hockey. Bill Masterton was a member of the Minnesota North Stars who met an untimely death on January 15, 1968, when he struck his head on the ice during a game. This trophy is dedicated to the memory of a man who demonstrated a high degree of the qualities for which it stands.

One player from every team in the league is nominated each year for this award. When they informed me that I was to be the 1983 winner of the trophy, it was with great pride that I realized I was being recognized for something other than a goal total.

The Bill Masterton Trophy is under the trusteeship of the Professional Hockey Writers' Association, and they flew Ardell and me to New York to accept the award. Mrs. Carol Masterton, a very gracious lady, made the presentation, and I hold the trophy in the highest regard.

That summer, I also had the honour of being inducted into the Blood Indian Tribe Range Patrol at an all-day affair at Standoff, Alberta. The celebration began with an authentic Indian meal in the chief's teepee, and the actual initiation ceremony was colourful and impressive, with chanting and ritual dances. The tribe's medicine man painted my face and then gave me an Indian name, Chief Weasel Rabbit. He explained that the name had come to him in a dream, and meant, to him, "swift and cunning." He presented me with an eagle-feather headdress, and I was then officially one of the tribe. The day finished with the passing of the peace pipe, and that alone made it an event to remember!

We had travelled a lot that summer, but when we received an invitation from the office of Prime Minister Trudeau asking us to attend a barbecue in honour of Prince Charles and Diana the Princess of Wales, it took us only seconds to make our decision. Our family, along with the rest of the world, had followed the courtship of "Chuck and Di" and had been among those who sat in front of a television at 2 a.m. to see their spectacular wedding. To be perfectly honest, we could hardly wait to see them in person.

When Charles and Diana arrived, they began their "walkabout," shaking hands along the way. Ardell and I were excited, just to be able to see this famous couple up close and never imagined that we'd actually have the chance to talk with them. Diana has a very easy manner, and as Prince Charles shook my hand, she looked at me and said, "With a moustache like that, you must be with the RCMP!"

I just smiled. "No," I said, "I'm a hockey player."

Charles interjected, "That's a very rough sport. I hope you're careful." And on they went, leaving me with a grin on my face from ear to ear. A great way to cap a great season!

12

RIVALS

"How could you ever lower yourself to do that?" some woman I didn't know asked me.

A lot of people have asked the same question, and I always laugh, but inside, I understand. I may have done some silly things in my life, but making a television commercial for the Alberta Fish and Wildlife people with Glen Sather, the coach of the Edmonton Oilers, was not one of them, despite what others may think.

Not many people realize that my relationship with Glen Sather goes back to my early days in hockey, when I was a student at the Calgary Booster Hockey School and Sather was one of the instructors, before he opened his own school in Banff.

If the truth be told, it was Sather who gave me my

first job in hockey. After I attended his school, Glen offered me a job—first as a phys-ed instructor, later as an on-ice instructor. We boarded at Sunshine Village those summers, and I was in charge of off-ice conditioning. Mostly, I took the kids on hikes and we ran up mountains. For me, it was the best of two worlds. A chance to work with good people and a chance to stay in great shape. I worked four years for Glen Sather, and I learned an awful lot from him, both by watching and listening.

When you consider the rivalry between the Flames and Sather's Oilers, the last thing you'd expect is for us to be in a commercial together; at least, that seems to be what the public thinks. The funny part is, the point of a commercial is to get a message out, and what better way to catch people's attention than by having an Oiler and a Flame on the screen together. I'm sure the Alberta Fish and Wildlife people were happy about the commercial, even if the hockey fans in Calgary and Edmonton were surprised at the "odd couple."

I still consider him a friend, although it's difficult, considering the rivalry between our two teams. Once, while Sather was playing hockey for the Minnesota North Stars, he threw an elbow at me. I just looked at him. He stood there with that Cheshire cat grin on his face—you know, the one you always see behind the Oilers' bench. There was a message in that grin: "We may be friends off the ice. But on opposing teams, friendships are put on hold."

Over the years, I don't think he's changed. He still plays by the same rules he did then. He's always had that air of arrogance about him, which throws a lot of people off and gets them riled. I think I probably understand him better than most, but that doesn't mean he doesn't upset me. I just don't get mad as quickly as other folks!

Like every other member of the Calgary Flames over

the past few years, I have made the Oilers and Sather the focus of my hockey existence. Because of the geography, because of the realignment and because of the strength of the Oilers, the annual success of the Flames is often judged by how well we compete against them. We feel that other teams have a clearer path to the Stanley Cup: We have to get out of our own division first, which means defeating the Oilers!

For a number of years, we seemed to be beating our heads against the Oiler wall. We could beat the Flyers once in a while; we could beat the Islanders; we played well against Montreal. But we couldn't beat those ?(*&*>:@#$% Oilers! And there was Sather behind the bench, smirking as always; afterwards, bad-mouthing Calgary or our fans or something, all in the name of rivalry.

After too many games and too many losses to the Oilers, the Flames developed something of a paranoia about them. You see, the Calgary–Edmonton rivalry isn't strictly about hockey. Hockey is only part of the larger picture. This rivalry is between cities, mayors, concert halls, Commonwealth Games and Olympic Games, the oil companies, theatres. It's a rivalry that dates back further than the life of the Flames or the Oilers.

As a kid, I remember hearing about the Calgary–Edmonton rivalry between the football teams. Even then, I was anticipating what was to happen later in life: I cheered for the Stampeders, not the Eskimos.

As the Oilers became Stanley Cup contenders, the rivalry between us grew stronger. We hated to play them because they were so good and so cocky; but at the same time, we liked to play them because we wanted to prove that we could turn everything around. This became the ultimate challenge for us.

The Oilers have become the main target of our schedule, sometimes to our own dismay. We always look ahead to meeting the Oilers, often forgetting about the team we have to play before them. It has cost us points in the standings, no doubt. But in the fans' minds, the Oilers games are the ones that really count. There's an electricity in the air that is really crackling by game time. We sense that anticipation and are ready to roll when the puck drops.

The games with Edmonton are more frantic and more intense than any others. To be honest, I was worried about them for a while. There was a time when the games were getting out of hand. Back in the last year we played in the Corral and the first year in the Saddledome, there was a hatred between our teams that surpassed anything I've ever seen. It wasn't just a battle to see which team won or lost; some nights, it was a battle to see who survived.

The fights became more frequent, the stick work more evident. The games grew longer. The situation just got out of hand, and I believe it was sad. In my own mind, I feel that the other team was more guilty then we were, but I'm sure both sides did their share. Still, you don't forget incidents like Mark Messier sucker-punching Jamie Macoun from behind or Dave Semenko kicking Tim Hunter. You can't forget the brawls, which both teams participated in. Mostly, all that's behind us now. Hockey between the Flames and the Oilers has gotten much better, and the games are without many of the incidents that marred our previous matches.

I am often asked about the violence in pro hockey and my answer hasn't really changed over the past few years. Violence to me is not the fighting. I see nothing wrong with a good clean one-on-one battle. It can be a release valve for emotions that can build up over the course of a game. The part of the game that worries me is the slashing, the butt-ending, the blatant high-sticking and the cheap crosschecks from behind. These infractions have to be recognized and dealt with more severely. I sometimes wonder too if the face mask gives players a false sense of security. Even though it serves a purpose of protection, it may give players a feeling of indestructibility and at the same time prompt them subconciously to carry their sticks just a little higher.

Our first playoff series with the Oilers, in 1983, was nothing short of a disaster. Despite losing the first two games in Edmonton, we came home for Game 3 hoping that being in the Corral would be to our advantage. I guess it didn't work. Nothing did that night for the Flames. We lost 10-2, with Wayne Gretzky setting a Stanley Cup record for most points in a playoff game. Frankly, I don't ever remember a longer game; it seemed like it took forever. I was injured and standing behind the bench to give encouragement, but how do you keep morale up when the other team is in double figures? I knew how Don Cherry must have felt coaching the Colorado Rockies! After everyone had written us off, we actually won Game 4 of that series, but we were blown out 9-1 in Game 5 and returned to Calgary with our tails between our legs. In a five-game series, we had been outscored 35-13. If there was a rivalry here, it certainly seemed one-sided.

If our series with the Oilers had proved anything, it proved how far away we were from competing with Edmonton. And again, if we couldn't compete with Edmonton, we couldn't advance out of the Smythe Division.

The fact that we lost as badly as we did led to a number of changes at the end of the season. Cliff Fletcher wasn't about to stand pat with a group that had been blown away by the team it has to be able to beat. The first deal came in early June, when winger Steve Christoff was sent back to Minnesota for centre Mike Eaves. It turned out to be a great deal for the Flames. Mike played his heart out every night and led by example. His enthusiastic attitude toward life and the game was infectious, and he has become an integral part of the Calgary Flames.

A few weeks later, we acquired Steve Bozek for Kevin LaVallee and Carl Mokosak. Bozek's speed and versatility would help us move up the ladder and compete with the Oilers. The same day the Flames made another deal, one which was bittersweet for me. We acquired my old teammates and friends, Steve Tambellini and Joel Quenneville, in exchange for Mel Bridgman and Phil Russell. But as thrilled as I was to have Tambi and Joel on our side, it meant saying goodbye to Rusty and Mel. We'd miss them both. Phil had a way about him that was easy and friendly, and Mel had given us a combination of toughness and hockey smarts. But it was a trade to increase our speed.

Unfortunately, though, Quenneville didn't last long as a Flame. Sixteen days later, he and Richie Dunn went to Hartford for Mickey Vulcan. The moves continued into early September, when the Flames signed defenceman Paul Baxter as a free agent.

Then, just before training camp was set to begin, Cliff Fletcher called me into his office. I wasn't sure what it was all about. "I know this isn't going to sit well with you," Cliff said, and I got a funny feeling in my stomach. "We've traded Guy Chouinard to the St. Louis Blues. Just wanted to let you know, before you hear it from someone else."

I was disappointed. Chouinard had assisted on almost half of my 66 goals the previous season, and I didn't want to lose him— as a centreman, as a teammate or as a friend. It was sad to see Guy leave. He was the best passer I'd ever played with, and he had a kind of honesty about himself and about the game that was so rare. He was gone, and to me it didn't seem fair.

Nonetheless, I was grateful to Cliff for the way he handled it. He's more than just a general manager. He's someone who cares about his players, their families and their feelings. He wanted to be the one to tell me the news because he knew I'd be disappointed. I've always appreciated that.

The new Flames, in their new home, sometimes played like the old Flames in their old home, achieving success with every team except the Oilers. In the 1984 season, we again beat the Vancouver Canucks in the first round of the playoffs, and once more we were set to play the Oilers in the Smythe Division final.

The first year we played the Oilers, expectations were high: The media had built up the rivalry angle, and everyone was expecting a long series. But we hadn't delivered. So as we prepared to play them for the second year, the press was predicting a short series. Some called the Oilers to win in four games. Those who were generous figured five.

That was the first time we surprised the Oilers. Going into the series, we figured we had to do several things right to beat them. We couldn't afford to make errors. We couldn't get caught in odd-man situations or allow them to wind up. We had to take a man-to-man approach in playing defence. And we had to have great goaltending. As it turned out, we had just about everything we needed.

After five games, the Oilers had won three. We returned home for Game 6, one that eventually went into overtime. Overtime is a different world, where everyone has his own approach. Some players want to sit back, hoping to capitalize on a mistake. Some look to be aggressive, hoping to pressure their way into a winning goal. Personally, I tend to take the bull by the horns and just go for it!

While with Toronto, I scored the overtime winner that eliminated the New York Islanders from the playoffs. And against the Oilers, I was in the right place at the right time. We had dumped the puck in the Oiler corner in overtime when Kevin Lowe tried to shoot the puck off the boards, out of their end. Carey Wilson was chasing Lowe and made him rush it. I managed to keep the puck in, and when I looked towards the net, all I could see was Eddy Beers wrapped up with an Oiler defenceman in front of goalie Grant Fuhr. I shot the puck on net hoping something good would happen. It hit Fuhr's stick and went between his legs. We had won! The Saddledome fans were going crazy. We were going crazy. It was the kind of night you never want to end.

But it wasn't over. The series that was supposed to be short was now a best-of-one. We felt so good the night we beat Edmonton; it was really too bad we had to go back to Northlands Coliseum to play a seventh game.

The seventh game was a strange one to say the least. Despite being outplayed, we were leading 4–3 halfway through the game, and it seemed like something, someone was on our side. Reggie Lemelin was playing unbelievably in goal, and the Oilers seemed shocked by the developments. Everything was going our way until Mark Messier crunched Mike Eaves into the boards. Mike was injured and didn't return. We also wound up losing two of our best point producers— Paul Reinhart and Al MacInnis— before the game was over. We were never really in the game again, and the series was lost.

Needless to say, we were disappointed. And we were even more disappointed when we saw how easily the Oilers beat Chicago and went on to win the Cup. We couldn't help but think, "That could have been us."

After going seven games with the Oilers and watching them win the Stanley Cup, we couldn't wait for another shot at them. Again they finished way ahead of us in the standings, but again we were hoping to catch them by surprise. Somehow the Winnipeg Jets stole the idea: They caught *us* by surprise, and our playoff season lasted four games. That year we lost to a team that was hungrier than we were. Maybe we were guilty of looking ahead to another series with the Oilers instead of concentrating on the one at hand.

Our loss to the Jets had not only riled the fans, but the media as well. They were bent on finding a convenient scapegoat for the Flames' problems. When you lose, the easy thing to do is to look for someone to blame, but I've always believed you win and lose as a team. A lot of people were pointing the finger at Kent. I didn't agree.

I'm not blaming it all on the press, but they certainly fuelled the fires when it came to Kent. They said he didn't care. They said he let the team down. My feeling was that a lot of people didn't understand Kent. I'd gotten to know him pretty well over the last couple of years, when I sat beside him in the dressing room, sharing good times and bad. Never for a moment did I believe that he didn't care. Kent cared; he just didn't know how to show it. He was immensely talented, but didn't know how to harness those talents.

The decision at the end of the season was that Nilsson had to go. On the day of the NHL draft, the Flames traded him to the Minnesota North Stars in exchange for several draft choices. The second-round pick, Joe Nieuwendyk, has shown an abundance of talent, and his potential to shine in the league is evident. Good trade or not, I was sad to see Kent go, not only because we had shared a lot of good times, but because of his talent. It's easy to make changes, but it isn't easy to replace guys like Nilsson and Guy Chouinard.

Every move we made had a purpose in management's mind: Each trade was made to make us more competitive with the Edmonton Oilers. That was the bottom line. It had to be. The problem now was, there was a third team involved— the Winnipeg Jets.

Heading into the 1985–86 season, the predictions were almost unanimous. Edmonton would finish first in the division, with Winnipeg second. We would finish third. Except, as always, it didn't work out that way.

The Oilers ran away with the division, as expected, but the Jets had all kinds of problems. We had both good times and bad during the regular season, the worst being an 11-game losing streak in December and January. It was then we knew that moves were going to be made, but to Cliff Fletcher's credit, he waited until the team was back on the winning side before doing anything significant.

Even when you feel that a trade is coming, it doesn't mean there's any less surprise when it actually happens. The deal we made for Joey Mullen was a shocking deal, if not for the number of people involved, then for the timing. We had played Edmonton that night and had trailed 4-0 before coming back to tie the game 4-4. We had a feeling of accomplishment as we headed back to the dressing room at the Saddledome. All of a sudden, one player was called out, then another, then another.

Bob Johnson walked into the room and told us what had happened. The Flames had acquired Joey Mullen, Terry Johnson and Rik Wilson from St. Louis in exchange for Eddy Beers, Charlie Bourgeois and Gino Cavallini. Eddy Beers had been my linemate and had sat beside me in the dressing room for a couple of years, and I was sorry to see him leave. I was happy for Charlie and Gino because the trade meant they would get a chance to play regularly, something they weren't getting in Calgary.

When Beers was traded, it meant the continuation of something of a tradition in the Flames' dressing room. We used to call his seat the jump seat, because so many players had been in it over the years. It didn't matter who wound up there, they usually got traded or were sent down. When Beers left, Terry Johnson took his seat. He lasted half a season with us. Now the seat belongs to young centre Brian Bradley, and we've told him to either solidify the seat or find another place in the dressing room. I think he'll solidify the seat.

As things turned out, it wound up as a good deal for both teams. Mullen gave us more scoring power. Johnson gave us toughness in front of our net. The three players who went to St. Louis gave the Blues more depth. And who would have thought on that night of February 1 that the Flames and the Blues would later wind up playing each other for a berth in the Stanley Cup final?

If that trade was a surprise, the second major deal that season caught everyone off guard. As a player, you like to try to anticipate what's going on with your team. We all knew the Flames were looking for a left winger, and the name that kept being mentioned was John Ogrodnick, of Detroit, who has since been traded to Quebec. We were nearing the March trade deadline, and because of the rumours, it was a tense time for our hockey club.

There are definite stages in waiting for a trade deadline. Two weeks before, everyone is a little uptight, thinking that perhaps they're the one who's going to be traded. The closer you get to the deadline, the more your attitude changes. You're still nervous, but you don't show it much. Everyone spreads harmless rumours just to stay loose.

The day of the deadline, we were playing the Islanders at the Nassau Coliseum. Nothing had happened the day before, and we thought that our team was set for the rest of the season. However, that morning, there had been a buzz of activity around the Marriott Hotel. Defenceman Steve Konroyd and forward Richard Kromm had been called to the rink early. We figured they were gone, but I still couldn't believe Konroyd would be traded. It had never even occurred to me. He was a steady defenceman who had been with the team before I got there. And I felt the same way about Krommer, who was a hard-nosed left winger. But in return we were getting John Tonelli, an experienced left winger and an all-star who had played a big part in the Islanders' four Stanley Cup championships. JT had been a Team Canada most-valuable-player in the 1984 Canada Cup, and we knew we were getting a player who could make the difference. The Flames were going ahead with their only plan: to move closer to the Oilers. And it was working.

If there was a reason we were creeping up on the Oilers, that reason was Cliff Fletcher, our general manager. As a GM, Cliff has so many things going for him. As well as going out of his way to make sure that the players and their families are happy and really caring about the people he employs, he has an ability few general managers have: He is able to separate himself from the coaching function. He's drawn a line between coach and general manager, and he doesn't step over it. Also, Cliff has always tried to deal from a position of strength. Instead of making a move during a losing streak, he's waited until the situation has improved and then taken advantage of it.

I don't think you'll ever hear anything bad about the way a player has been treated by the Calgary Flames. You might complain about ice time or how you're utilized but not about the organization. Cliff has gone out of his way to make everyone feel comfortable, and he's treated his players fairly and honestly. He's the main reason we moved up and the reason we played for the Stanley Cup.

13

THE STANLEY CUP FINAL THAT WASN'T

I've been through a Stanley Cup, a Canada Cup, a Challenge Cup, a Memorial Cup and a number of cups of coffee over the years, but none will ever compare to a seven game series we played that didn't even have a name.

Oh, there were nicknames— the Uncivil War, the Battle of Alberta, the Airbus Series— but none fitting for the division final that was played between the Calgary Flames and the Edmonton Oilers over a two-week period in 1986. Everyone said it should have been the Stanley Cup final and, considering that we won the series, we should have been the champions.

The Calgary-Edmonton series was unlike any other. I don't think I'll ever play again in a series where the level of concentration was so high, where the games were so fast, where the intensity never let up. Even the players sitting on the bench could appreciate the spectacle they were involved in. Some writers have called it the greatest series ever played. Right down to the final seconds of Game 7, the outcome was in doubt, and I guess that's the way it was meant to be.

The series began differently for us than previous ones against the Oilers. For starters, they had eliminated Vancouver the same night we knocked off Winnipeg, so both of us were starting out with the same amount of preparation time. And when you give Bob Johnson preparation time, he takes advantage of it.

The amount of work we did prior to Game 1 in Edmonton was incredible. We watched tapes concentrating on what Edmonton players are apt to do in certain situations. We had meetings. We practised. And, as a diversion, he brought in two college goalies and had them wear Oiler shirts in practice. Those who don't know the game may scoff at a move like that, but it sure broke the tension for us.

Heading into the series, Johnson had given us a definite game plan on how to beat the Oilers. The rest was up to us. We had to execute it.

The key to our plan was the first ten minutes of every game. We didn't want to get behind early, and we were told to concentrate on not being scored upon in the first segment of the game. This turned out to be our greatest weapon: In six of the seven games, we scored the first goal, and it seemed to throw the Oilers off somewhat.

We were told to stay out of the penalty box. But it was more than that. We were told to take a different approach to playing against Edmonton. If there were an altercation, we were to back away and not get involved in pushing matches. The strategy was to let them be the bad guys; if they started something, fine, but let them start it, not us. I think that attitude frustrated the

Oilers and kept us fresher because we weren't losing our strength by pushing and shoving.

Some players had individual assignments. Colin Patterson, for example, was told not to worry about offence as long as he made sure Jari Kurri didn't score. That proved to be a successful strategy, and Colin earned billing as one of the league's best checkers. Joel Otto's match up against Mark Messier also proved a winner; Joel was able to match Messier, check for check and draw for draw. And it was a team assignment to keep up with Coffey and Gretzky. We just couldn't allow them to wind up.

It seemed that no matter what we were assigned to do, it worked. Except for one problem: Grant Fuhr, the Edmonton goaltender, who may be the best in the game today. Had it not been for Fuhr, it wouldn't have been a seven game series. We probably would have won in five. Fuhr was unbelievable, and I'd be lying if I said there weren't nights I left the game wondering how to beat him.

Before the series began, there seemed to be an aura about it. I didn't know what it was, I just knew it was there. And the series began with a difference because of it.

Our team's president and general manager, Cliff Fletcher, rarely comes into our dressing room before games. He's always believed that coaches coach and managers manage. Sometimes after a game he'll walk in and talk to you for a second or two, but it's usually just a pat on the back or asking if everything is all right. Before Game 1 of the Oiler series, Fletcher surprised the Flames' players by appearing in the dressing room about an hour before the game, giving a speech that would have rivalled Knute Rockne. I wish I had taped it. All I know is that, after hearing it, I was ready to run through the dressing room wall to get to the ice.

"Unless we win this series, we've gained nothing,"

Fletcher said. "They will give us no respect. Respect will only come when we finally knock them off."

Just over a minute into the first game, I scored on a great pass from John Tonelli. We led 1–0, just like we were supposed to. Then 2–0. And things kept getting better. We won Game 1.

They won Game 2. We won Game 3, they won Game 4. We won Game 5, they won Game 6. Never have I been involved in such a roller coaster of emotions. Each time we were poised to win the series, we had a setback. Every time it looked like they were about to take over, we came back. It was hockey at its finest, with the momentum flying back and forth and the adrenalin rush never stopping.

The key for us was to keep our emotions in check. Everywhere you went in Calgary or Edmonton, people were talking about nothing but hockey. It was as if time had stopped and all that mattered was the game.

I have to hand it to Bob Johnson. I don't think I've ever seen better coaching than he did during that series. CJ, as the players call him, did everything he could think of to keep the tension low. He wanted guys to concentrate on the task at hand but not become obsessed by it. There's a fine line there, and it's important for a coach to understand the difference.

CJ did it mostly through his practice sessions. One day he'd have goalies with Oiler jerseys on. Another day he took us to the top of the Saddledome to watch a few of our teammates practise Oiler breakout tendencies. There was CJ, near the roof of the Dome, and his assistant Bob Murdoch was down on the ice setting up the drill. The two were yelling back and forth at each other, and neither could hear what the other was saying. It was very funny to watch, but at the same time, the message got across, which to my way of thinking is good coaching. Not only did we pick up some pointers from the exercise, we had a good laugh at the same time and released some of the building tension.

So much happened so quickly between Games 1 and 6, it's hard to remember it all. But I think our spirit was captured by a couple of things that took place in the second game of the series.

Flames' assistant trainer, Al "Little Bear" Murray, was standing behind the bench at the Northlands Coliseum when Gary Suter was checked into the boards. Suter, who uses a costly aluminum stick, was hit by an Oiler, and his stick went flying into the stands. Little Bear's first reaction was to get the stick back, not thinking much about the Calgary-Edmonton rivalry. He jumped into the stands to retrieve the stick, but the fan who had it wouldn't let go, and an altercation began.

Al Murray may not be the biggest guy in the world, but for his size he sure is a tough little beggar. Knowing that his son could take care of one guy, but not 17,000 Oiler fans, Bearcat decided to join him. The stick escaped unscathed. But Bearcat, defending his family, returned with torn ankle ligaments and wore a cast for the next several weeks.

Symbolically, I think that said something about the Flames: We were ready. We weren't about to back down. It also showed how keyed-up we were on the bench. Trainers play a significant part over the course of a season and get just as hyped-up as the players do. To me, that incident showed the determination we felt as a team.

Another contributing factor that no one could begin to measure was the fan support. After Game 2, with the series tied 1–1, we were pleasantly surprised to see the turnout of well-wishers who met us at the airport on our return from Edmonton. Following Game 5, leading the series 3–2, we returned to a terminal jampacked with fans as ecstatic as we were. It was then we realized the series just wasn't for us as a team, but for all of us as a city. The pride of Southern Alberta was at stake.

More than anything else, we were motivated by the fear of losing as we headed into the seventh game. And there truly was fear in our dressing room. You'd want to sleep at night, but you couldn't. You'd want to have your pregame sleep in the afternoon, but sleep wouldn't come. You'd be tired but not tired. I don't know if we were hungrier than the Oilers, but we had come this far, and no way did we want to walk away as losers. Like Cliff Fletcher had said, if we didn't win, we wouldn't get any respect. The meeting before the seventh game wasn't as long as usual. By then, everything that needed to be said had been said. Now it was up to us; execution was most important.

Normally our dressing room is not quiet: Guys are joking around, music is playing. But that night was very different. Guys were at the rink three hours before the game, trying to act as if they weren't nervous. Players who generally are dressed five or ten minutes before warmup were ready an hour earlier. And the odd thing was, no one was talking to anybody else. The music was off. The dressing room was silent. It was time for Game 7.

What impressed me most about Edmonton in the series was the fact that they never quit. They just kept coming at us. We wanted something so damn badly and were afraid to lose it. We wanted to put all those years of frustration, all those years of being beaten by the Oilers, behind us. But every time we took a lead in the series they came back. Until time ran out.

We went up 2–0. They tied it 2–2. Neither side was ready to give in. And then we got the winner.

In years to come, Perry Berezan may come up with an inventive way of describing the winning goal he was credited with. Maybe he'll say he took the puck over the blue line, made one move and beat Fuhr with a brilliant wrist shot. Or maybe, he'll say it was an end-to-end rush with him beating all five skaters and then deking the goalie. I'll leave it to Perry; I'm sure he'll come up with something good! Nevertheless, the goal is now famous. Famous in Calgary; infamous in Edmonton.

Berezan dumped the puck into the Edmonton end and came off on a line change. Fuhr stopped the puck behind the net, and defenceman Steve Smith hurried back to get it. I followed Smith behind the net, chasing him out the other side, hoping to make him rush the pass. Smith's cross-ice pass never got to the intended receiver. The puck hit Fuhr's leg and bounced into his own net.

Coming out from behind the net, I watched what had happened. It didn't seem real. I couldn't believe it. I let out an enormous yell. As soon as I got back to the bench, I started screaming, "It's meant to be. It's meant to be. It's got to be a sign!" On the bench, I had to tell Perry about the goal he had just scored, the biggest one of his life. He didn't even see it happen. Maybe I *will* help him develop that story about how he scored; it'll be a good one!

To this day, I feel badly for Steve Smith. If you're going to lose a seventh game, you want it to be on a great play. I did feel sorry for him, but I wouldn't want to change anything.

I've thought about it a lot, and I still don't know who's to blame for the goal, if anyone. But I think that goal proved that we were destined to win. In our minds, we knew we had outplayed the Oilers. That goal didn't tarnish our victory, and although some people have said that we fluked past the Oilers, I don't believe that for a second. Not only did we outplay them, but after taking the lead in Game 7, there was plenty of time left for them to score and tie it up, forcing overtime.

Frankly, I don't care how the win is construed by others. Regardless of who thinks what, we played a helluva series, and we won what may have been the greatest series every played.

The strange part of Smith's goal into his own net is that we almost did the same thing a few minutes later. Neil Sheehy almost banked a puck past Vernon, but somehow it stayed out. Another good sign. And we managed to hang on, which wasn't easy against the Oilers.

I was on the bench when the game ended. They had come at us pretty hard in the final three minutes, but Vernon kept making those big saves. The last faceoff of the game came with four seconds left on the clock.

Time stood still for a moment. As the clock ticked off the seconds, we stood at the bench staring at the clock, willing the buzzer to sound. We watched the final faceoff, barely breathing. The clock finally ran out. We had won!

We poured over the boards, yelling and screaming. It was a feeling like I've never had before. Everywhere you turned, someone was screaming, celebrating, hugging. It was an incredible scene. And we indeed had something to celebrate— something we'd never done before.

What made the victory that much sweeter was the fact that we had humbled them, somewhat. No matter what we had done in the series, no matter how well we had played, I still got the impression they didn't respect us. They never considered us a threat.

The Oilers had rubbed salt in our wounds long enough, and the hurt was over. They had been gloating for years, and now we had beaten them. Not only had we beaten them, we had outplayed them. And yes, there was shock on their bench when they lost. I don't think that any of them ever believed, even for one second, that we were going to win. And that's why the victory was so sweet.

On the flight home to Calgary that night there was a feeling of pure joy and relief. The stewardess came back and told me that someone in the cockpit wanted to say hello. Our neighbour, Bruce Watson, was the air traffic controller on duty that night, and he had radioed the team plane to pass on his congratulations. The pilot let me talk to Bruce, who told me that the plane behind us was loaded with Flames fans coming from the game. Kidding, I asked him to radio back to the plane and tell them to have a beer on us! Bruce said, "Tell them yourself, Mac, I'll patch you through."

On the approach to Calgary, our pilot came over the speaker and told the team to take a look out the window at Barlow Trail. The cars were backed up for miles, past McKnight Boulevard. And what's more, there were 20,000 people waiting at the airport to welcome us home. God, what a feeling. We had beaten Edmonton and won the hearts of all Calgarians.

I didn't sleep that night. I couldn't. I kept playing the game over in my head, celebrating in my mind.

The only problem with beating Edmonton was that we didn't have time to relish the victory and what it meant. I'll always wonder if our struggle against St. Louis in the next series was due to the fact that we had to shift gears so quickly.

There was no time for us to savour our victory, one we had been working toward for years. No time to pat each other on the back, to share our feelings with each other, lay the series to rest. After our games with the Oilers, we not only needed a rest physically, we needed it mentally as well.

We lost Game 1 against a St. Louis team we really believed we could beat without a whole lot of trouble. We lost our edge in that game, and suddenly the Blues were doing to us what we had done to Edmonton.

But, we knew that if we lost to St. Louis, it would diminish our victory over the Oilers. After giving away the home opener, we bounced back against a well-disciplined, well-coached club and led the series 3-2 after winning the fifth game at home. Then we took a lead in the sixth game, and it looked like it would be all over.

I don't know if we panicked in Game 6 or if it was something else. I think we were playing the "prevent defence" used in football, trying to protect a lead. We led 5-2, and before you knew it, it was 5-5 and we lost 6-5 in overtime.

Talk about numbness setting in. Reality has a way of shocking you. All I could think about on the long plane trip home was, "Thank God we have another chance." We knew we had blown it. We were just lucky it wasn't Game 7.

That was the attitude we were trying to take. We knew we had screwed up, but the thinking was, let's make sure it doesn't happen again. We wouldn't have been human if we weren't nervous going into Game 7. But we won it, barely, and were on our way to the Stanley Cup finals. Having already played a series against Edmonton that felt like the finals, I'm not sure there was enough left to play another one. But we were damn well going to try!

Some people have said that when we lost Game 6 in St. Louis, we lost the Stanley Cup. But I can't think that way. The only way I can look back and be satisfied is to remember that even if we had had those two extra days to prepare for Montreal, we still would have run out of steam in the finals. It just would have happened one game later.

14

SO CLOSE
I COULD
TASTE IT

I glanced up at the clock in the Olympic Saddledome and watched helplessly. Time was running out on my dream. As I sat on the bench, each second that ticked off the clock was like a stab through my heart. We were losing the Stanley Cup, and dammit, I didn't want to lose.

All I wanted was to see my name alongside the names of my Calgary Flames teammates, engraved on the Stanley Cup. The Montreal Canadiens were leading by a 4–1 score in Game 5 of the 1986 Stanley Cup finals, and four minutes remained in an incredible season.

After Steve Bozek scored to bring us within two goals and Joey Mullen scored to make it 4–3, I still sat on the bench, waiting to hear my name called. I kept think-ing,"This isn't the way this story is supposed to be writ-ten. Who screwed up the final chapters, anyway?" I couldn't believe or accept that we had come this close, playing a team we could have beaten, and that it would soon be over.

Time ran out. In the final four minutes, my name was never called. I never stepped on the ice. Deep down, I was devastated. I wasn't even given a chance to tie the game. After 13 years in the league, and having already scored 11 goals in that year's playoffs, I thought at least I deserved that much.

You figure that maybe this is your last shot, maybe your only shot, at winning the Cup, and in the back of my mind I'll always wonder if I could have made the dif-ference. That's one question I'll never be able to answer.

As the final buzzer sounded, I didn't know what to think. We left the ice to the overwhelming sounds of the Saddledome fans chanting, "Thank you Flames, thank you Flames." I thought about the fans, the people making up that amazing sea of red; about being in the finals and losing; about not playing in the final minutes. I was so drained of energy I wasn't sure if I wanted to be left alone or have someone to talk to.

It was a crushing feeling to have come as far as we had and have it end the way it did. I couldn't talk. I couldn't explain my true feelings. I wanted to say so much and so little, all at the same time. I made no at-tempt to fight back the tears that flooded my eyes.

I'm not sure anyone who hasn't been in this position before could totally understand it. I even have trouble explaining it. Some players never get their chance. This had been my chance, and it was over. We had lost.

I had looked on this as the opportunity of a lifetime, a dream that could come true. And I was angry about it, angry we had lost. Angry at coach Bob Johnson for not playing me in the final minutes. Angry that something we wanted so much, something we deserved, wasn't ours. One day, I hope to have the chance to write that final chapter again, the way I want to write it.

The Stanley Cup final went so quickly we barely had time to consider what was happening. We played an explosive series against the Oilers that went seven games. With no time to savour our victory, we had to meet the Blues. We barely beat St. Louis, and then it was time to start the final. I'm not sure if we were ready for it, but ready or not, we came out and won Game 1 at home. The emotion and excitement of being in the final carried us through the first game. It almost carried us through the second, too.

Actually, we would have won Game 2 had it not been for Patrick Roy, the Canadiens' goaltender, who went on to win the Conn Smythe Trophy. The Canadiens won that second game, 3–2, in overtime, with Brian Skrudland scoring nine seconds into the overtime period. The momentum had shifted.

We had already lost Carey Wilson, Gary Suter and Colin Patterson to injuries. But still, we had others who could play. However, the coaching staff thought certain players were getting tired and wanted to insert some fresh blood. They began making lineup changes and adding new faces regularly in the finals, much to the surprise of the Flames players. Chemistry is very important to a team, and when you've gone through as much as we had to get to the finals, the bond between the team members is particularly strong. All of a sudden, players who had been a big part of our success throughout the playoffs were no longer in the lineup. It wasn't the reason we lost, but it didn't help.

The Canadiens won Game 3 handily. Everyone was saying that we must be a tired hockey club by now. And I suppose that was true. But we never thought of ourselves as tired; we'd come so far, and we sure weren't going to let a little fatigue stop us now.

Roy won the Conn Smythe, but to me the Montreal defence was really their overall tower of strength. Roy was just the final line. Gaston Gingras, who had bounced around the league a little bit, played the finest I've ever seen him play. The same was true for Rick Green. And Larry Robinson, as always, played a stand-out series. Those three guys—in fact, the entire Montreal defence—played as if they were seven feet tall and four feet wide.

It became very frustrating in Game 4, when we executed our game plan to perfection. We wanted to get into an old-fashioned low-scoring game, and that's exactly what happened. Two periods ended, and neither had scored. Then Claude Lemieux, who had been a royal pain in our side, made it 1–0 with about half the period left. Normally ten minutes is lots of time to get a goal. But in those final minutes, I'm not even sure we had a scoring chance. That's how much they frustrated us. That's how well the Canadiens played defensively. We tried to hang on as long as we could. There just wasn't enough to hang on to.

When you lose the Stanley Cup, your only thoughts are that you've been defeated. There's little consolation in having had a good season or in the victory over Edmonton, which was the greatest playoff series I've ever been involved in. You can't remember how much you've accomplished, the mountains that were climbed along the way.

But to understand the end of this season, you have to start at the beginning. For us, the beginning was in Moncton, where the Flames had decided to hold training camp.

Before the season even started, I felt I had something to prove. My past few seasons had been injury riddled, and I was determined that this year would be different. I wanted to play all the games; of course, I had no idea then that "all" meant 80 regular season tilts and 22 more in the playoffs, the most any team had ever played in the history of the game.

I wasn't alone in my desire for a good year. Doug Risebrough, co-captain of the Flames, was in the same position. Let's face it, our careers were in question at the time. Riser had played only 15 games the year before; I had played 37. There was speculation that we were both finished. Doug and I talked a lot about people writing us off, and I think we became closer because we were in the same situation. For us, it wasn't only a challenge; it became an obsession. The onus was on us to come back, although no one was really expecting it.

Bob Johnson runs a busy training camp. If you're not skating, you're in a meeting. If you're not in a meeting, you're taking aerobics class or yoga or nutrition classes or something else. But the camp in Moncton was different, especially for the older guys. We were told to take our time, to take it easy, to go slow and make sure we were ready to play when it counted. I got into my first exhibition game hoping to do just that. Instead, I wound up in a fight.

I threw a punch at Jere Gillis of the Vancouver Canucks and ended up dislocating my thumb. I'll be honest, even though I can usually hold my own, I'm not one of hockey's great fighters. "Even my four-year-old knows to tuck his thumb in when he throws a punch," teammate Paul Baxter kidded me.

I had torn some ligaments in the thumb, but I was lucky and it wasn't as bad as I originally thought. The problem was, it was my shooting thumb. My right hand has helped me survive 14 seasons in the NHL; I learned my wrist shot as a boy, practising against a basement wall, and it's been a skill I've been proud of ever since.

Now, my shooting thumb was injured, and our first game was only ten days away. The day before the season started, on trainer Murray's suggestion, I took a hockey stick to the hospital, where they moulded a new cast, designed so that my hand was in the right position to shoot. In the first game of the season, I scored a goal and had three assists, and the guys had one bit of advice for me: Wear the cast all the time.

The best part was, I hadn't missed a game, although it sometimes seemed as though the team's trainers, Bearcat Murray and Bobby Stewart, were the reason I was playing. Sometimes I felt like Humpty Dumpty: They were putting the pieces of me back together again. But I was playing, and that's what I had set out to do.

We had a strange regular season. Every time it looked like we were reaching a certain level, we'd fall back again. In January, we hit rock bottom. We were losing, although we weren't playing that badly. Then we were losing and playing badly. We lost five in a row. Then it was seven. And quickly, panic set in. We knew we were in trouble, but no one was admitting it. Everything we had done right earlier in the season, we were doing wrong now. We tried to stay optimistic. But as time and the losses went on, we were expecting something to happen—a trade, a major change, a coaching change, something.

After seven losses we thought we had bottomed out. But towards the end of what eventually was an 11-game losing streak, we were one ugly team. We lost 9-1 at home against Hartford and knew we couldn't go any lower. We were totally disorganized and trying our hardest not to look at each other and point fingers. We tried to remain positive. It wasn't easy.

It became a matter of survival. We kept waiting for something to happen. But the only thing that happened was that Mike Vernon, the goaltender, was called up from Moncton. Nobody thought much about the move at the time, figuring that goaltending wasn't the reason we were losing.

The strangest part of the 11-game losing streak was that we didn't drop in the standings, which tells you something about the kind of year other teams were having in the Smythe Division. We stayed in second place, while Winnipeg, Vancouver and Los Angeles battled for the last two playoff spots. Every time we thought we had problems, we'd look at Winnipeg, who had knocked us out the year before, and realize we weren't so badly off.

Eventually, we put the losses behind us, and we were able to look back at the losing streak and laugh, something we couldn't have done at the time. And when defenceman Jamie Macoun went to accept an award at one of the monthly Molson Cup luncheons, he said, "I didn't expect to be here. Then again, after losing 11 games in a row, I didn't expect CJ (Bob Johnson) to be here, either!"

We finished second in our division, which meant we would play Winnipeg in the first round of the playoffs. Bumps and bruises aside, I managed to play all 80 games of the season, and Risebrough wound up playing 62 games.

As we were preparing for the Winnipeg series, Coach Johnson put together a line that was quickly dubbed the "Not-Ready-for-Retirement Players," with Risebrough at centre, John Tonelli on left wing and me on right. I don't know if it was because of age, experience, styles or the excitement of the playoffs, but we clicked as a line right off the bat.

We were supposed to be a defensive line, but in the Winnipeg series everything went right for us offensively all the way to the final goal in overtime. We had won the first two games quite handily, with the Jets having all kinds of trouble in goal. They used three goalies in the first two games and started their fourth goalie, an unknown kid named Daniel Berthiaume, in Game 3. Well, Berthiaume was unbelievable, and we had all kinds of trouble beating him. We should have put the game away early, but because of Berthiaume the game went to overtime.

Now, going into overtime is tense, but to the "Not-Ready-for-Retirement Players" it was exciting! Some people called our line "old"; we referred to ourselves as "experienced." We'd show the kids how it was done. We did. A few minutes into overtime, JT, Riser and myself got it together. Riser threw the block, JT feathered the pass and I tucked it past Berthiaume. We scored, won the game and yelled at those "kids" on the bench, "Bring on the Oilers!"

15

SPECIAL
INTERESTS

Some of the most memorable games of my life were games I didn't really play in: the Special Olympic Games. My interest in the Special Olympics dates back to my first season with the Maple Leafs and has only grown stronger as the years go by.

I guess it all started when a man named Harold Smith invited Jim McKenny and me to the Beverley School in Toronto. There mentally handicapped people were being given the opportunity to learn independence and grow accustomed to living on their own. I was interested in what they were doing and was happy when I was asked to represent the Maple Leafs at the 1974 Special Olympics Summer Games in Winnipeg.

I arrived in Winnipeg in the early afternoon and met

some of the athletes before returning to the hotel for the night. The athletes, coaches and volunteers all stayed in the same hotel, and, of course, there were rules: bed by 10 p.m., breakfast at 7 a.m. Well, we finally got the athletes to sleep about 1 a.m., and I fell into bed exhausted.

I was dead to the world when there came a knock on my door. It was 6 a.m., and someone was knocking at my door. I heard giggling and laughing, and I'm thinking, "What's going on?" When I opened the door, there were some boys from the Beverley School. They had convinced the hotel cook to give them toast and juice, and they brought me breakfast in bed. It was a simple gesture, but it made me realize how much they really had to give. I knew then that this was the start of a long friendship with a group of warm-hearted, generous athletes.

I've learned so much from the Special athletes, but the more I'm around them, the more I realize how much they give of themselves and how little they ask in return. All they want is to be treated like everyone else and given a chance. So many of them are sports fanatics. They can name you every player on the Maple Leafs and give you their statistics. In Winnipeg, they knew I only had 14 goals my first season, and still they were willing to bring me breakfast!

There's a saying about the Special Olympics: "Once you've been there, you're hooked." And I was definitely hooked after my first real contact with the athletes in Winnipeg. And once I showed an interest, a wonderful man named Harry "Red" Foster made sure it wasn't passing. Red Foster was a man of many passions, but none stronger than his passion for the Special Olympics. He is no longer with us, but he is by no means forgotten. Red was an original. There will never be another like him.

He made sure my involvement with the Special Olympics increased over the years. When we were living in Denver, the Special Olympics in Canada were just getting established. Procter and Gamble sponsored a cross-country promotion for Special Olympics, and it was the first time a major company had gotten behind them. Red phoned me one day in Colorado just after the season ended and asked if I could come back and do a commercial for the Special Olympics. I told him I'd be honoured to help out.

"What's your schedule like?" he asked.

"When do you need me?"

He said he needed me on Monday. This was Friday. With Red, it didn't matter "when," as long as "when" was "now." He was the kind of guy who could get something done in a hurry. As I got to know him better, I became more involved in the Special Olympics. And the cause was just beginning to grow.

The Special Olympics then were different from the Special Olympics today. There was very little promotion, very little sponsorship. But more and more, people began to realize how important sports are to children. Sports foster self respect and self esteem. When you have a handicapped child, the natural tendency is to protect him or her. It took a long time for people to realize how beneficial athletic competition can be for handicapped children.

In the beginning, the public wasn't recognizing that. Red Foster was one of the many people responsible for making people aware of these special children and their needs. He made sure there was something challenging for these kids to do. I know because I've seen it—because I've shared it. I've seen so much in my years with the Special Olympics, but the major events are what you remember most. For example, the International Games in Baton Rouge, Louisiana, are something I'll never, ever, forget.

I was just one of many volunteers involved with the

Canadian team. First, we went to London, Ontario, where a short training camp was held for the Canadian athletes. It was our first chance to meet each other, and, after a send-off barbecue, we left on two chartered airplanes for Baton Rouge. It was a fun trip: A good many of the athletes had never been on a plane, and some of them had never been away from their parents before. So it was like stepping on new ground for them, setting new goals.

Once we arrived in Baton Rouge, we prepared for the opening ceremonies. We had it all worked out. The Canadian team would enter, come down the track, walk by the reviewing stand, on which Eunice Kennedy Shriver, Ted Kennedy, Frank Gifford and our own Red Foster stood, and tip our red and white caps in tribute.

It didn't exactly work out that way. Imagine, if you will, 150 Canadian Special athletes walking into Tiger Stadium at Louisiana State University; suddenly, 70,000 spectators are on their feet, cheering, clapping, stamping. We weren't five feet into the stadium when the hats were off and the athletes were waving. They didn't stop waving as they marched all around the stadium

One young guy, with tears in his eyes, said to me, "Can you believe it? They're all cheering for us." Athletes were cheering. Coaches were crying. People in the stands were crying. And they were all tears of joy, tears of respect for such a wonderful gathering of fine athletes.

The Special Olympics has a motto: "Let me win, but if I cannot win, let me be brave in the attempt." The Games at Baton Rouge proved that the Special athletes take that motto seriously, as have all the Special Games, I've ever been involved with.

I wish I could share all the heart-warming things that have happened during my involvement with the Special Olympics but if I did, I'd be writing a book that would never end. The stories aren't always easy to relate. The feelings they stir up certainly aren't, either. But from those International Games in Baton Rouge, there are so many stories to tell.

We were at the gymnastics competition. Athletes are entered at these Games according to handicap and ability. One small, mentally disabled boy, with only stumps for arms and legs, arrived at his side of the mat in a wheelchair. His coach picked him up and placed him on the mat. There was dead silence in the packed gym. The boy completed two forward rolls and a backward roll and then sat up as straight as he could. His coach picked him up as if he were a champion, and he waved to the cheering crowd. There were tears in his coach's eyes and you could see the boy saying to the camera, "Hi, Mom! Hi, Dad!"

That kind of courage and spirit displayed by the youngster shows you what the Special Olympics are all about. It really makes you sit back and think.

There have been so many times when these athletes have made us all cry. First, because their effort is so impressive. Second, because their love and understanding are so great. Third, because of their honesty, which is next to none. They just don't pull any punches. The funny part is, and it goes back to being sports fans, if they think you've played a brutal game, they'll tell you so. You laugh and cry with them because they are so honest. And when you get emotional, the tears aren't out of sadness or pity; it's just that you can't believe they have that much inside them and are willing to share it. The tears you cry at the Special Olympics are tears of happiness, tears of pride. It's those times that are the most memorable.

What I remember most vividly, though, are the personal experiences, the athletes who have touched me deeply. I think back to a bowling competition in Ottawa in 1980. I was watching this young guy from the North-west Territories, and he was having all kinds of problems. I thought I had better go over and console him. "Don't worry about it, " I told him. "The most important thing is having fun."

"Hey, don't worry about me," the youngster said with a big smile. "I got a chance to come to Ottawa. My friends don't even know where Ottawa is."

With these kids, just having a chance to compete means they've already won. And because of all this, my perspective changed. Vince Lombardi was wrong. Winning isn't the only thing: Participating is. More than a decade of involvement with the Special Olympics has changed my approach to sports. I see competition differently now. Maybe I'm more able to accept defeat than I was before. I think I was better able to handle a blow like our Stanley Cup final loss after having worked with the Special Olympics.

We'd given everything we had to win the Stanley Cup—and not just one or two players, but everyone. Yet, despite the effort, we still lost. Earlier in my life I think I would have been devastated by a defeat like that. At the time, I was crushed, but I recovered. I accepted it. Special Olympics have enabled me to put life ahead of sports. It alters your perspective; it means the little things are, in fact, little.

I've travelled all across Canada and to various centres in the United States with the Special Olympics. But the Games I think I was proudest of were the ones in Calgary in 1986. I guess you take pride in the things that take place at home, where you are witness to just how much planning, hard work and volunteer hours are involved.

The Calgary Committee put forth their bid for the Games at the Floor Hockey Tournament in 1984, and from that moment on, Calgary '86 was underway. Chaired by Don Taylor, a board of dedicated and professional people freely gave of their time and expertise to ensure that the Games would be a resounding success. The call went out for volunteers to work at the Games, and the response was phenomenal. Over 1000 people signed up for 800 jobs, proving that Calgary truly is a city that cares. Corporate sponsorship was unparalleled, with the Royal Bank leading the way followed closely by the Burns Foundation, the Canadian Progress Club and the NHL.

Ron and Marg Southern provided the internationally acclaimed Spruce Meadows for the opening ceremonies. The stands were filled. The roads were jammed. And the opening ceremonies had to be delayed until everybody could get in. More than 10,000 spectators showed up, Mila Mulroney opened the Games, and long-time friend of the Special Olympics, Grant McEwan, offered good wishes.

That was a festive week. The Flames hosted a cocktail party for the athletes' parents. The Stampede Board put on a real western barbecue, and cowboy hats were presented to the athletes. It was quite a sight, seeing all the participants walking around in various-sized cowboy hats, dancing to a "down home" country and western band. But everyone came together then as they always do at these events. It was, not to overuse the word, a very "special" time.

That week Jim Peplinski and I were at a floor hockey match when a boy sitting next to us started talking to us. He was the goalie for the Saskatchewan team, and he teased, "You'd never score on me, you know! You'd never be able to blow one by me."

The next day, we arrived at the floor hockey court in time to jump over the boards and congratulate the Vancouver and Saskatchewan teams, who had just finished a game. Quinn Wirth, the young goalie we had been talking to the day before, was lying in the Saskatchewan net. "Come on, Quinn, get up! They didn't wear you out, did they?" I called to him.

"What do you mean?" he laughed. "I can't."

I was silent.

Finally he realized. "You didn't know!" he laughed. He thought it was all a big joke. His coach came and put Quinn in his wheelchair. He had no control of his legs and played goal by kneeling in front of the net.

"Sometimes they get a few high ones on me," he chortled. "But they never beat me low."

Once in a while we still hear from Quinn. He writes to both Pepper and me. You don't forget guys like Quinn Wirth. Ever.

That same week, the track and field competition opened, and it was a miserable day. It rained like crazy, and officials were threatening to call off that day's meet. The athletes, coaches and timers were all soaked. But the athletes weren't complaining; they were there to compete. And compete they did. The volunteers were amazed at their resiliency and ability to adjust to the conditions. Had it been an ordinary track meet, it would have been called off.

When you're as committed to something as I am to the Special Olympics, you want to involve your friends. I haven't had to work very hard to get my teammates interested in the Games: The Flames' management and players have been involved since the team moved to Calgary. The Flames Annual Golf Tournament has raised more than $150,000 over the last six years for the Special Olympics.

There are many NHL players and referees who give their time to the Special Olympics, and we get a lot of credit for our work. We don't want credit. We're not the heroes here. The athletes are the heroes. The coaches and parents are the heroes. I'm involved once in a while. They're involved every day. They're the ones who make it work. I have the utmost respect for the parents. Sometimes we don't get the whole picture, since we see only one side of the Special athletes. We see them at the fun events, the good times. We aren't there day to day or through the tough times. You have to admire the parents and the coaches for all they do for these children.

I don't know if I'll ever be able to adequately explain what the Special Olympics have meant to me. It's something I feel— something that's there and always will be there. As far as I'm concerned you can't emphasize the word "special" enough. I cannot remember doing anything more satisfying in my life.

The Special Olympics have given sports a new meaning for me. They've given me a new outlook on life, and they've most certainly helped me a tremendous amount with my own children. Sometimes people are afraid to show their true emotions, especially in public. Not Special Olympians. They believe it's right to show how much they really care. I sometimes wish we were all a little more like that.

I have been given more by the Special Olympics and the athletes who participate in them than I could ever begin to give back. I'll always be grateful to Red Foster, who encouraged me to continue his dream.

16

HAROLD
AND
KING

As I waited for the opening faceoff, my eyes darted in the direction of the famous box at the north end of Maple Leaf Gardens. It had been boarded up. It hit me then, harder than it had hit before: King Clancy was dead.

I've always made a point of looking to the box where Harold Ballard and King Clancy sat watching the Toronto Maple Leafs play. When I was a Leaf, and something interesting happened on the ice, I'd always look that way just to see Harold and King's reaction. I wanted to know what they were doing, what they were thinking. They were a lot of things, but most of all they were entertaining.

After I left the Leafs, each time I returned to Maple

Leaf Gardens I continued my habit of checking their box and waiting for their reactions. But when I looked up on January 26, 1987, it had already been covered over with boards. It just didn't seem right. Later, I was glad to hear they were opening the box again. It should be open, keeping the memory of King Clancy vivid in the minds of those he touched, those who knew him and those who watched him.

King was one of the first people I met the day I was drafted. When I was taken over to the Leafs' table at the NHL draft, King took me under his wing and never let me fly on my own until I was ready. Harold wasn't around during my first year with the Leafs. That was his year out of hockey.

But King was there whenever you needed him and in my case, that meant quite often in the early years. If you had a problem, he was the guy to talk to. He came equipped with words of encouragement and wisdom. And sometimes, in a different sort of way, he'd give you advice. King would come by, telling stories the way only he could, and when he left, you realized there was a message in what he said. Instead of calling you aside to berate you, he'd find another way to get his point across, and to me, his methods were most effective.

The more trouble I had each year, the more frustrated I became. I was feeling the pressure, not only to score, but to get what had been advertised as my "big shot" away. Every chance I had, I wanted to unload the "boomer." But nothing worked right.

Finally, King came to me and said, "Let's not worry about that big slap shot of yours. Let's not even worry about the wrist shot. Why don't we start at the other end; when you've taken care of that, everything else will come together too." He was so right! One thing about King Clancy: When it came to hockey, he knew what he was talking about.

Harold returned to the Maple Leafs scene in time for

my third season, in his predictably outspoken manner. In one breath, he wondered aloud if Inge Hammarstrom would crack any eggs if he played with them in his pocket, and where he could trade his high-priced help from the west—me. He was telling the fans he wasn't satisfied and telling me he wasn't happy.

In a way, I knew what Harold was saying, and it bothered me. But it just made me work harder to prove him wrong. However, in Inge's case, Harold's comments had a more devastating effect. Inge was such a sensitive person that he took what Harold said to heart; he saw it as a personal slur rather than as an off-the-cuff comment. I think if Harold had made the same observation about someone else, it wouldn't have hurt as much. But in Inge's case it was devastating and he didn't know how to deal with Harold's remarks.

It was times like that when King proved to be the perfect buffer for Harold. King was always around. Game day, practice day, it didn't matter. If there were something that had to be talked about, King was there. If something went wrong, it seemed as though King was the guy who could straighten it out, carrying things off in his casual way. He'd come into the dressing room and say something like, "Can you believe what Harold said about McDonald?" But the way King said it, nothing appeared as bad as it was. Having him around was like having a full-time good luck charm. King had a twinkle in his eye, a little of the leprechaun magic and lots of that good old Irish blarney.

At the time, we were still getting to know Harold. We kept hearing about this gruff, growly old bear, and not much of what we heard about him was good. The papers were quoting him with some pretty lethal comments. However, my theory has always been that you have to make judgements for yourself.

One on one, Harold Ballard is a nice guy who really cares!

No, that was not a misprint. It's true. Not that long ago, Ardell was talking to the father of a recently traded Leaf player. He said to her. "I bet Lanny and I could swap all kinds of stories about Harold."

"Lanny has a lot of respect for Harold," Ardell replied.

"He what?" the player's father said.

Ardell repeated herself. The conversation ended.

To me, there are two Harold Ballards—the one you read about in the newspapers and the one I got to know while playing for the Maple Leafs. More than anything else, Harold is misunderstood. Because of what happened in Toronto, a lot of people have the impression I had problems with him. Even when I was playing for the Rockies, Harold and I would talk for a few minutes whenever we'd play the Leafs, and I made sure he got a cigar when each of our children was born. The press tried its best to keep the controversy going, but there was never any animosity between us. Harold treated my family and me well. The biggest problem I ever had with him was his choice of general managers! And later on, even he questioned his hiring of Punch Imlach.

It doesn't seem to matter what I say, people don't believe me when I talk about Harold Ballard. They see only the public side of the man. Sure, he says things he shouldn't say and does things he shouldn't do. He's a little more outspoken than most owners. But there are really only a few things that are dear to Harold's heart. His best friend, King Clancy, was one of them. His hockey club, the Maple Leafs, is the other.

To Harold, being on the front page of the sports section was the only place to be. It didn't matter what was going on. Harold wanted the Leafs to be page-one news. The Leafs were his baby, and he wanted his baby to get as much attention as possible. At first, he battled with the Argos for the headlines. Then came the Blue Jays. But if the Leafs kept the front page, what was said about them didn't really matter.

Harold could trash his players as easily as he could praise them, and often he hurt people by what he said. But I don't believe he ever meant his comments to come across as harshly as they did. What is it they say about being harder on the ones you love? Well, that's the way Harold was. It was his team, and he figured he could say whatever he wanted. In some ways I don't blame him, but it's easier for me to say that now; I don't play for the Leafs any more and I'm several years removed from being hurt by his comments.

Harold had the blustery reputation he has today when I first joined the Leafs, and as the years went on, he became more and more outspoken. No matter what you want to say about him, you have to admit he is entertaining. He's colourful. He loves the limelight and likes nothing better than to shock people. Sometimes I wonder if we all would act that way if we owned something that we loved as much as Harold loves his Maple Leafs.

For all but my first two years with the Leafs, Harold and King travelled with the team on the road. It was strange to see one without the other, and it just didn't seem right if one of them was missing. We actually looked forward to them being on the road with us, and at the time I thought all owners travelled with their team.

The friendship between Harold and King was something special that actually brought smiles to the guys' faces. When we travelled, Harold carried a stash of chocolate bars, and King, always looking out for Harold's best interests, would stand at the front of the plane trying to give away as many bars as possible. "If you don't eat them, Harold will," he would joke.

They really did have a relationship that was second to none. There were the odd trips that Harold took when

King didn't come along, and Harold always looked lost without him. It was as if he weren't sure what to do without King at his side. When King lost his wife, Harold urged him to get back on the road with the Leafs. He did, and I think that helped him deal with the grief. They say that opposites attract, and Harold and King were one of those perfect matches.

A lot of people think Harold's only interest is making money. I don't believe that to be true. Anybody out there who thinks Harold considers the Leafs only as a business obviously doesn't know him. He cares about the Leafs. And he cares about his charities. The only difference between the two is that he doesn't want publicity for what he does outside hockey. That's the side of him not many see.

When King Clancy died last November, I was saddened to lose an old friend, but my next thought was, "How's Harold?" They were so close, you had to wonder how Harold would survive without his sidekick.

I was out of the Flames' lineup with an injured knee when King died, and I guess in a way the injury was a blessing. Cliff Fletcher was going to the funeral and asked if I would accompany him. I was honoured to do so, and it meant a lot to me to go back to Toronto, having a chance to say goodbye to a friend who had been so good to me. I left King's funeral with a strange feeling. It's never easy to eulogize someone like King, and no matter what was said about him, no matter who said it, you wanted them to say more. He went with grace and dignity, the way a man like him deserved to go.

On my next trip to Maple Leaf Gardens, I automatically looked around for King Clancy. Without him, the building didn't seem right to me. And it didn't seem right that the box where he and Harold alway sat, side by side, was closed. King would have wanted it open, just like he was.

In a naive sort of way, I expected there would be King Clancys and Harold Ballards everywhere I went in hockey. Of course, I never found anything quite like them again.

17

ME AND
MY
MOUSTACHE

Paddy Boutette used to call me Fur Lip. A sportscaster in Toronto referred to it as a picket fence on my face. It reminds my dad of a corn broom. It's been the target of many cartoonists, and Mike Barnett says it is to me what 99 is to Wayne Gretzky. It's long, it's wiry and sometimes out of control, but it's my moustache, and I like it.

It's been part of me for so long that it's hard to remember a time I didn't have it. Even when my own kids look back at pictures of me without my moustache, they sometimes think they're looking at pictures of Darryl Sittler. No offense intended, Sitt.

When I started growing a beard back in the summer

of 1974, I had no idea that anything other than whiskers would come of it. I was driving home to Medicine Hat after my rookie season in Toronto and didn't bother taking the time to shave on the trip. The whiskers started coming in, and I decided to see what kind of a beard I could grow. By mid-summer, I had a full red beard, even though I knew I would have to shave it off in the fall when I went back to Toronto— at that time, the Leafs didn't allow beards.

After having the beard all summer, I really hated to get rid of it, so instead of shaving off the whole thing all at once, I did it in stages. First I had a goatee, but it made me look sinister. I tried a Fu Manchu, but that wasn't for me either. Then I tried a short moustache— a normal moustache if you will— and that's how it stayed for three years, neatly trimmed and just sitting there under my nose.

Then I saw Sparky Lyle, and he had just about the greatest moustache I'd ever seen, huge and bushy. Sparky was a relief pitcher for the New York Yankees, and I was always hoping that the team would have to call him out of the bullpen; I sure admired that 'stache!

It was then I decided, "That's for me!" I know now that I should have asked Sparky's advice, because mine didn't turn out the same; it has a mind of its own, and no amount of wax can train the damn thing.

I never dreamed of what was to come. My moustache has become part of me— part of my identity— something I can't imagine ever 'etting rid of. I've been offered money by various companies to shave it off during a commercial, my father has tried to bribe me into shaving it and Uncle Jack has threatened to take the sheep shears to me. But my moustache, to me, *is* me. And, I found out, my moustache is me to a lot of other people too.

In some ways it's a diversion, giving people something to talk about. In the 1986 playoffs, it became almost a trademark of the Flames: People were selling red moustaches in much the same way the North Stars used to sell little green Dino Ciccarelli dinosaurs. Everywhere you went, people were wearing bushy red moustaches made of wool or fun fur or cotton batting—anything that was fuzzy and furry. And there were even T-shirts sold in Calgary during the finals showing the Stanley Cup sprouting a big red moustache. It's almost become part of the personality of the team, but it wasn't until I was traded to Calgary that the moustache started to mean something to anyone other than me.

It was during my first full season with the Flames that Mike Barnett, of CorpSport International, a sports management company, approached me about becoming a client. I had known Mike when he owned the Sports Page Restaurant and Bar in Calgary, and I had always been impressed with his business savvy and people skills. Mike is a real professional, and he didn't want me to get involved in one-shot promotional deals: His idea was to work on a long-range plan of action, establishing a working relationship with companies and designing on-going campaigns to promote their products.

I thought it might be interesting and lead to one or two endorsements or commercials, but I never dreamed it would be as much fun as it has been or bring me into contact with so many terrific people. Another plus has been the chance to get out into the business world, which is particularly valuable for an athlete. Sometimes you get caught up in thinking that the world revolves around your sport, and the commercials I've done have given me a peek into the "real" world, an opportunity to learn what makes companies tick.

The first business that Mike aligned me with was Calgary Copier, a company that deals in Canon home and office machines. Calgary Copier is owned by a fine gentleman named Russ Parker, who also owns the

Triple A professional baseball franchise in Calgary, and he's been part of the sporting world for a long time. What started out as a purely business relationship between Russ and me has evolved into a friendship that I'll always value. He's a great guy who is proud of his businesses, and justifiably so.

In the Apollo Muffler series, Chris Stavenjord, the creative director, came up with a unique way of selling mufflers: He has four of us doing a song-and-dance routine in the middle of the Apollo Muffler shop. In another, we're dressed in white tuxedos doing a fifties' "do-wap" kind of number. It's crazy, it's fun and it's certainly an unusual way to sell mufflers. But it works! These are probably the commercials that I'm most identified with and take the most ribbing about. It must be because I'm such as great singer and dancer! The truth is, one of the back-up dancers in my first Apollo spot told me it was a good thing I could skate, because I sure didn't have any rhythm. I was crushed by his comments; I had practised for hours and days; with my daughters as coaches, trying to perfect the steps. However, it took us dozens of retakes to finish the commercial, complete with bloopers that we'll laugh about forever. People still ask if it's really me singing.

That same year, Ardell and I were approached about doing advertising for a local furrier in Calgary, Benzing Furs. Like the Apollo ads, they took a light-hearted approach. Though the furs were beautiful, I think it may have been hard to tell where the coat started and my moustache left off!

I've also really enjoyed doing the series of commercials for Alberta Fish and Wildlife. Growing up on a farm, I learned to enjoy and respect the outdoors, and being able to do something for my own province is important to me. I've done this commercial alone, with Ardell and the kids and, most recently, with Glen Sather, the coach of the Oilers. What I'm proudest of are the results of those commercials: One of the messages that runs throughout the series is that you should get permission from a landholder before hunting on his land, and then respect that land as if it were your own. Since the advertising program started the number of complaints about trespassing hunters has been drastically reduced. That's what I call getting the message across.

Some commercials fit the moustache perfectly. I did one with seven kids for Carnation's "Chocolate Moustache" drink; at the end of the spot, after taking a drink, all the kids sprouted big red moustaches. It was a great concept, but even my daughter, Leah, was hesitant to take her first sip of the drink: She wasn't completely convinced that the commercial was trick photography and wondered if she'd end up with a fuzzy moustache on her upper lip!

Because of my name and their name, I always wanted to do a commercial for McDonald's. I never thought it would happen, but when the chance came to make a cameo appearance in one of their ads, I was thrilled. The first shot was of a youngster, about six years old, and me, sitting in a booth and eating fries. I was kind of nervous waiting for the shot to be set up and figured I should try and calm the little boy down too. At my reassuring words, he looked up and said, "Oh, I've done lots of commercials, there's nothing to be nervous about."

We've also had some good laughs because of my moustache. The referee credited me with what was to be my four-hundredth goal; later I discovered that Eddy Beers had tipped the shot into the net. I had the goal stats changed to reflect Eddy as scorer, and the next day a cartoon appeared in the paper. Dave Elston, a cartoonist with the *Calgary Sun*, made light of the situation surrounding my "not four-hundredth" goal: He showed the entire team on the bench with moustaches, and the caption read,"It was Eddy's idea, Lanny. If anyone tips your 400th again, no one will know the difference!"

Dave Elston also did a cartoon when our first son was born. It showed two doctors chatting outside the hospital nursery. "Rumour has it that this is the hospital Lanny McDonald's new son is at." The bottom frame of the cartoon shows three babies in nursery cribs, one sporting a large moustache.

I hope that in some way my moustache has helped the causes that I really believe in and work hard for. Ronald McDonald House is a project that is dear to my heart, and at least with my moustache no one can confuse me with Ronald McDonald, although lots of youngsters think we're brothers. When I visit the Alberta Children's Hospital in Calgary, my 'stache gives me an easy introduction to the patients and leads to some good-hearted banter from kids that need a bit of cheer.

A shaving-cream company once asked if I would shave off my moustache for a commercial, but I turned them down. Shaving off my moustache would be like shaving off my identity. I don't think I'll ever mow it!

To this day, I've never met Sparky Lyle, but I certainly thank him for the inspiration. Without him, I don't know what I'd look like today. And as my sister-in-law, Marilyn, says, at least the moustache hides my big nose!

18

TEAM McDONALD

Every team in the NHL has a yearbook. Sometimes they call them media guides. In it are the names, statistics and specifics about the men who play on that team. This is my media guide. And this is my team: Team McDonald.

There were no particular qualifications to make Team McDonald, but the fact is, all the members are guys I once played with. Talent wasn't necessarily a prerequisite. This team is simply made up of the players who, somewhere along the way, left their mark on me. They may have been friends, they may have been linemates, they may have been great competitors. Sometimes, they were all three.

As in the case of most NHL yearbooks, when there is

an outstanding player, he gets top billing. And my condensed media guide will begin with a most special person, a most special player:

Darryl Sittler, Toronto Maple Leafs

What can you say about someone who became as close as a brother?... When times were good, he kept things in perspective; when times were bad, he knew how to help you find that confidence you had let slip away... A Maple Leaf to end all Maple Leafs... It was a shame to see controversy surround him the way it did, a shame that he didn't remain a Maple Leaf... The Leafs were in his heart and he lived and died for the club... My centre for five seasons, but more than that, my best friend... You make friends in hockey, but few like him... Also a great player and a great centreman... Would rank among the top agitators in the history of hockey... Subtlety was his specialty... Knew when to play a practical joke but always stayed out of the line of fire... Also knew when to be serious and how to say the right thing... Helped me, in and out of hockey, more than he will ever know... Probably the most important man I've ever played with.

GOALTENDERS

Glenn (Chico) Resch, Colorado Rockies

The greatest... A true ambassador of the game... Always takes the time to chat... and chat... and chat!... Can turn a yes or no answer into one of 25 words or more... Always knows the "scoop": His dream was to be the oldest player in the league... He's made it!... I'm proud to have been a teammate and get to know a great guy like Chico.

Reggie Lemelin, Calgary Flames

A true friend... On the list with Jamie Hislop of all-time best roommates... All-star card player... The most normal goalie in the game... Guys tease him that he's so normal he should have been a forward... Fastest feet in hockey... My partner on the road with the Flames; we've spent many hours sipping a cool one with our GM hats on... We've helped each other over some rough times in the game... Thank goodness for a friend like Reggie.

DEFENCE

Jim McKenny, Toronto Maple Leafs

Howie... Truly one of the funniest men ever to play... No one lived or played as hard... With Jimmy, there was never a dull moment... The king of the one-liner... Always had a comeback line... Once, during an all-star game in Chicago, he made a bad pass to Phil Esposito. After the play, Phil said something to Jimmy, and when asked about the comment in a postgame interview, Jimmy joked, "He was telling me about the blonde in the fourth row."

Borje Salming, Toronto Maple Leafs

BJ... The King of Sweden... One of the best talents ever to play... Something set him apart from the rest of the Europeans— more confidence and more guts... If he wanted to say something in the dressing room, he'd say it... A fierce competitor... Despises losing... In a battle of any kind, I'd want Borje on my side.

Rob Ramage, Colorado Rockies

Rammer... Tremendous talent, but tried to carry the whole weight of the Rockie franchise on his shoulders... That was too much for a young guy, or any guy, to handle... Career improved when he was traded to St. Louis and became the all-star defenceman everyone knew he could be... One guy who really did deserve a break... even if he does like Mexican food for breakfast!

Phil Russell, Calgary Flames

Rusty... John Wayne on skates, slow-moving, slow-talking... Great team captain who took the position seriously... He really cared about his fellow players and their feelings... Was a costly euchre partner, but he probably says the same thing about me.

Jamie Macoun, Calgary Flames

Cooner... The Rebel... Marches to the beat of his own

drummer... Considered the most "different" Flame, but mostly he's misunderstood... Also known as Crazy Legs; from a standing start is probably the fastest man in the league... Stick around him and you'll have fun... Tells us he's our off-ice captain... Enjoys the game and knows how to enjoy life away from the game, too.

Joel Quenneville, Toronto Maple Leafs, Colorado Rockies, Calgary Flames (almost)

Uncle Herbie... Taught our daughters to dance... Shared some great times in Denver... Knew how to make me laugh—Ark! Ark!... It's great to see him becoming an all-round player and a kingpin on the Hartford defence.

Charlie Bourgeois, Calgary Flames

Chuck, or Chas... Could be Mayor of Moncton!... A real team guy who kept everybody loose... Don't ever get into a war of words with Charlie, he'll slay you with those one-liners... One of a kind... Great to see him be a regular and play well in St. Louis... No one deserves it more.

FORWARDS

Ron Ellis, Toronto Maple Leafs

Chuvalo... The kind of guy you think of as your hero... A true credit to the sport... Taught me a lot about the position we played... Great to have on your side... Took time with young players in Toronto... A great family man.

Dan Maloney, Toronto Maple Leafs

Satch... As tough a player as has ever played the game, and no one worked harder than he did... Wasn't afraid to grab somebody in the dressing room if he thought they weren't pulling their weight, and he'd lay it on the line... Difficult to play against when he was with Detroit... One player everyone was glad to have on their side.

Walter McKechnie, Toronto Maple Leafs, Colorado

Rockies, Everywhere

McKech... Had a career that seemed to last forever... He didn't run out of seasons, he ran out of teams... No matter where he went he enjoyed himself; and so did the people who hung around with him... A prankster of some repute... One of the guys who made life enjoyable in Denver... A good friend and a good companion.

Steve Tambellini, Colorado Rockies, Calgary Flames

Tambi... A true gentleman... Highly skilled player who handles the puck as well as anyone... A great friend, not only of mine but of my family... We all look forward to spending time in the summers with the Tambis... Still waiting for that elusive trip to Hawaii!

Jack Valiquette, Toronto Maple Leafs, Colorado Rockies

Hector Head... A real card... How could you help but like him?... He's funny, his laughter is infectious and his perennial smile could brighten any day... Used to kid us that he was so slow on skates he could deke the same guy three times on one rush.

Jim Peplinski, Calgary Flames

Pepper... Never short of words... A major-league practical joker—I may have to play a few more seasons just to get even with him... Has done outstanding work in the community... Works as hard off the ice as he does on it.

Colin Patterson, Calgary Flames

Heater... The Rodney Dangerfield of hockey... Not only does he do a great impression of Rodney, Colin doesn't get "no respect" either... Probably one of the finest defensive players in the game today.

Dan Quinn, Calgary Flames

Quinner... Cocky and often obnoxious, but I still like him... Has enough confidence for a whole team... Sad to see him leave Calgary, but it was the best thing for him... He's proving he belongs.

Guy Chouinard, Calgary Flames

Chou, which is pronounced "shoe"... He used to say the fans weren't booing, they were "chouing"... On the all-time humour team with Jimmy McKenny... The ultimate passer... The man most responsible for the best season I ever had... Glad to see he's now coaching and staying in the game he loves.

Doug Risebrough, Calgary Flames

Riser... The steal of all steals in a trade... What he gave the Flames was far beyond whatever they could have given up for him... May be the best leader I've ever played with... Added more class to the organization... A guy I really relate to because we play along the same lines... Believes in an eye for an eye and a tooth for a tooth.

John Tonelli, Calgary Flames

JT... Looks like the Tazmanian Devil or a whirling dervish on skates... The third member of the "Not-Ready-for-Retirement" line, along with Riser and myself... We were thirty-three and thirty-two and he wasn't yet thirty but got lumped in with us anyhow... The kind of guy who could grow a beard between periods... Brought experience and a knowledge of winning to our Stanley Cup drive.

Nick Fotiu, Calgary Flames

Sir!... A prankster who could win Hall of Laughs honours... Once was caught putting baby powder in the locker room hairdryers... Has a sense of knowing when a team needs a lift, on the ice or off... Has done a tremendous amount of community work throughout his career... Knows when to be tough... Popular with fans and teammates.

Joey Mullen, Calgary Flames

Schmo... No one realizes how much talent he has... Major-league scorer... Tough little guy, too... When you grow up playing on rollerskates on concrete in New York, you learn not to fall down much!... Pep says everyone should have a Joey Mullen doll.

Gary Croteau, Colorado Rockies

Crow... Hard worker who had to endure some tough injuries at the end of his career but never complained... Enjoyed the game and the people... Was very good to us in Denver and made it fun... made the transition from hockey to the business world look easy... Prepared well for his retirement and never looked back.

Mike Eaves, Calgary Flames

Bear... A breath of fresh air... His friendship and sincerity are next to none... A great family man; like the Pied Piper with children... His juggling kept everyone entertained... A real team man who took everything in stride: If it happens, it's meant to be, and you go from there... After talking with Mike, nothing ever seemed as bad... My life is richer for knowing Mike Eaves.

My team wouldn't be complete without mentioning the rest of the 1986–87 Calgary Flames.

Paul Baxter

Hardnosed defenceman who liked to throw the big hit in open ice... A good team guy who really helped the young defencemen.

Perry Berezan

"All-Canadian Boy"...The boy next door, a versatile player who, like Bozie, can play any forward position... Plays the keyboard as well as Elton John does.

Steve Bozek

Valuable asset to any team... Can play all three forward positions... Plays a mean guitar and could start a rock band with Perry.

Mike Bullard

Anyone who likes Alf has got to be all right... Has an abundance of natural talent... Hell of a hockey player.

Tim Hunter

Does what he has to do, when he has to do it... Through his own hard work is probably one of the most improved players in the league.

Hakan Loob
Calgary's answer to Mats Naslund... Loads of talent... Short but Swede!

Al MacInnis
Rounding into an all-star... By far the hardest shot in pro hockey... I always tease him that he'll have to be "Little Mac" because I'm Mac!

Joel Otto
Shy and quiet off the ice... Big and strong on the ice... Great on face-offs and in the front of the net.

Paul Reinhart
Has natural talent and can play defence or forward... It's nice to see him playing so well after his serious back injury.

Neil Sheehy
His personal phone book is thicker than a dictionary... Should have a phone surgically attached to his ear... Has steadily improved since coming to the Flames.

Gary Suter
He tells us that, pound for pound, he's the toughest hombre around... Young version of Phil Russell... Slow-walking, slow-talking dude.

Mike Vernon
Everybody likes Mikey... Hometown hero... Won his place by taking us to the Stanley Cup finals.

Carey Wilson
Secretly wants to be a stage comedian but has the sickest jokes in the league... Maybe that's why he's going to be a doctor!

Brian Bradley, Kevin Guy, Brett Hull, Joe Nieuwendyk, Gary Roberts
"The kids"... The up-and-coming future of the Flames— and it looks bright!

This is my team, and if you don't agree, I guess you'll have to write your own book!

19

ARDELL
AND
THE KIDS

"I'd like to thank Ardell and the kids." The phrase was part of any interview I did, and Billy Clement used to tease me unmercifully about always saying it. But it was true. Much of my success and all of my happiness are due to my lady and our wonderful children.

The first time I saw her, I knew she was for me. She was sixteen, I was eighteen; she was a figure skater, and I was a hockey player. Sound like a movie? Boy meets girl. They fall in love. They get married and live happily ever after. It makes a good movie, but it makes a better reality.

I used to stand behind the pillars at the Medicine Hat Arena and watch her practise. From the first time I saw Ardell, I wanted to ask her out, but it took me a long time to get up the courage. I finally did—sort of—and it was definitely a first date to remember.

One night I scored two goals in a game, and I knew Ardell was there. I made up my mind that if I scored a hat trick, I'd ask her out. "If I score a third goal tonight," I said to our stick boy, Michael Farmer, "can you please find Ardell Moyer and ask her if she'll wait for me after the game?" It really was my lucky night; just a few minutes later, I scored another goal. Instant panic set in. "What have I done? What if she says no? What if she says yes?" I raced for the bench, hoping to catch Mike before he went to find Ardell, but I was too late.

Our actual date was a bit unusual. After all, two's company, three's a crowd and five makes a group. My parents and brother had come to town for that game and decided to stay for the evening—the same evening I finally had a date with Ardell. We all had a good time. At the end of the evening, I took Ardell home and went in to meet her parents. When I walked in, Ardell's father was standing by the door. He's a big man—about six-foot-three, 255 pounds—looking up at him, he seemed even bigger.

"Nice to meet you, Danny," he said.

I looked up at this enormous man and thought, "No way am I going to tell him my name isn't Danny!"

Once Frank and Lucille got my name straight and I had been "OK'd" by Ardell's sisters and brother, their good friend Eric Lloyd, who was chief of police, ran my name through the C-PIC for a final approval. I must have checked out, because only then did I become a regular fixture at the Moyer home. Frankie soon taught me some of his tricks of doing "fine" yard work, and I think he had a method to his madness. He was grooming me for the day when he could sit back and relax, knowing I was taking care of the yard his way!

I grew up in a household that was hockey-wise and

found it unusual that the Moyers knew little about the game. I had to give them a crash course in the finer points of hockey, and I'm not sure they were that interested, but everyone went along with it anyway. Frankie wasn't as concerned about hockey as he was about this young whippersnapper who was taking up his little girl's time. He wondered what I was going to do with my life after I finished fooling around with junior hockey. Now, when I have daughters of my own, I can understand his concern, and he and I compare notes on the way to raise daughters.

Ardell was still in high school, grade 11, and even though she attended all my games, she was often not allowed to go out with me afterward if it were a school night. I'd take her home, she'd toddle off to bed and Lucille and I would sit up analysing the game. I think that was the start of a very special relationship that I have with Lucille. I may have taught her a lot about hockey, but she taught me a lot about life: about people, about leaving your options open, about getting a handle on things. She is a warm, generous lady and an astute businesswoman, and she gives me some very good direction and guidance. She has always treated me as a son, and I love her like a mother.

Between home games and road trips, our dates during the hockey season consisted mainly of after-game burgers or telephone conversations. I think the only school dance we ever made was at Ardell's graduation. The year Ardell graduated from high school, I graduated from junior hockey. We both felt very mature, but we knew we were too young to be married; that fall I headed for Toronto, and Ardell went to college to start her degree in education. Near the end of training camp, when I knew I had made the Leafs, I phoned Ardell to ask if she could be there when I played my first NHL game. She couldn't miss an exam, but she and Lucille did see my first NHL goal. As a matter of fact, they were probably the only two people cheering in the Montreal Forum when I scored that night.

The romance continued— at long distance rates! Frank and Lucille wanted to take their family to Hawaii for Christmas, but the kids voted for a trip to Toronto instead. That visit just reinforced how much I missed Ardell and wanted to spend the rest of my life with her. We were engaged on February 1, 1974, and married on July 12, 1975.

I'll never forget Ardell coming down the aisle on her father's arm. She looked radiant, and I couldn't keep my eyes off her. St. Patrick's Church in Medicine Hat was full of family and friends, but I could only see Ardell, the girl I loved. When Father Shahoun pronounced us man and wife, I knew it was the most important moment in my life.

We honeymooned in Bermuda and the Bahamas. I thought I'd impress her: I took her golfing, but we had to stop on the fifteenth hole, because I ran out of golf balls; at a clam bake, I tried the limbo and fell flat on my back; I told her that if she tried kite skiing, I'd film it for posterity, but the camera ran out of film. Nevertheless, the marriage survived!

Back in Toronto for the start of my third season with the Leafs, the papers were full of trade rumours and vicious comments about me and the way I was playing. But it didn't seem so bad because I had someone to help me cope with the pressure. Whenever I heard those comments, Ardell would tell me to ignore them, tell me to believe in myself and to play the way I knew I could. Even though the trade rumours about sending me to Atlanta were disturbing, I knew that if it happened, we'd go together.

A month into the season, my hockey career started to turn around, and I really attribute the change to Ardell. She was working with Andra Kelly, teaching the blind to skate, and I helped with her class one day. Seeing the determination and dedication of those blind skaters on the ice brought me up short: Here were people who were challenging their handicaps and confronting their fears, trusting someone to help them face the unknown. They worked hard to develop, and the process was slow, but they never got discouraged. They met the challenge head on. It made me look at my own situation. As a result, I just dug a little deeper to meet my challenge, and with Ardell's encouragement, November was the start of it all.

Our first year of marriage was one long honeymoon. It was fun showing Ardell Toronto: We must have tried every restaurant in the city, and I know we saw every movie released during that year. We strolled Yonge Street, poked around Yorkville and shopped and shopped and shopped. We had all those "dates" we'd missed!

The day that Ardell told me that "we" were pregnant was the day before I left for the Team Canada training camp. I was so excited I wanted to shout it from the rooftops, but we decided to keep the news to ourselves for a while. At least, that was the plan. Off I went to Montreal for training camp, and hard as I tried, I couldn't keep it a secret. When Ardell arrived ten days later, everyone seemed to know we were expecting. She teased me that I must have been walking around meeting people, and saying, "Hi, I'm Lanny McDonald, and my wife is pregnant!" So much for keeping it quiet.

I was having a great season, we were in our first house, and we were preparing for a little "Mac." I was on a roll, headed for a 50-goal season, and Ardell didn't want me to miss any games. The Leafs had a road trip just before the baby was due; I went with the team, but I was determined that, regardless of the hockey schedule, I'd be back for the baby's arrival. That was one date I wasn't going to miss! I had checked airline schedules all over continental North America and had routes planned, "just in case." Our first stop on the road trip was St. Louis. I scored two goals, phoned home and Ardell was fine. We went on to Denver. Again I called home. "There's a plane at 4 p.m., and I can be on it." But Ardell said she was fine, to go ahead and play. At 5 p.m. I got a call from Ardell, saying that maybe I should fly home after the game. We were going to be parents— soon. But she said she'd wait until I got there. I checked the flight schedule. I could leave Denver at 2:30 a.m., fly to Chicago and catch an early morning connection to Toronto. I played the game and scored my fortieth goal of that season. Then I checked in at home. Lucille and Wendy Sittler were just taking Ardell to the hospital— I'd better hurry. As fate would have it, the plane was late leaving Denver, and I missed my flight from Chicago. Now what? I called ahead for a car to be waiting, flew to Buffalo and made like OJ Simpson through the airport. Then I picked up the rental car and drove like hell to Toronto. I sprinted across the hospital parking lot, dashed into Ardell's room and said, "Did I make it on time?"

Andra Erin Moyer-McDonald was born at 5:10 that afternoon by Caesarean section. It was St. Patrick's Day, 1977, and our little Irish girl was gorgeous! The miracle of birth is not to be equalled: To know that you're responsible for moulding and shaping a little life is extraordinary. We looked at our baby daughter and knew that we'd give her everything we could, especially our love.

The next day, a nurse came into Ardell's room laughing about some fool who had run across the hospital parking lot clutching a four-foot pink elephant. They were chuckling about this when I walked into the room carrying that same four-foot elephant. The nurse looked at me and said, "First-time father?"

Ardell and I seemed to be awfully "baby illiterate," and thank god Lucille was there to show us the ropes. Mom stayed with us for the first month after Andra came home from the hospital, and we were all certifiably baby crazy. Andra quickly became the centre of our lives, and we couldn't wait to take her home to Medicine Hat and show her off.

Andra was precocious, always a real little lady, and she had all kinds of attention from everyone. We spent our summers in Medicine Hat, and, surrounded by two aunts, her grandma and poppie and us, Andra quickly learned to converse with the adult world. She started talking at an early age, and her first words were in complete sentences. Ardell's sister, Marilyn, can take full credit for Andra's love of reading and the arts. Marilyn talked to Andra as if she were a grown-up and read to her for hours. When Andra was older, Marilyn often took her to concerts and art exhibits. I remember when Le Ballet Jazz, from Montreal, was performing at the local college. Marilyn had a ticket for Andra. Ardell and I weren't sure that a three-year-old would enjoy it, much less be able to sit through even the first half of the performance. But off they went, with a promise to come home if Andra didn't like it. We should have known: Andra not only loved it, she danced in the aisle through the second half! It really is amazing what children can absorb at such an early age.

Andra is now ten, a very mature young lady who is always looking out for her younger brothers and sister. She's a little girl who really cares about people.

The craziness and pressures of the Imlach days in Toronto were made easier for Ardell and me by the fact that we were expecting our second child. Leah Bevin was the bright spot during those first weeks I was a Rockie; she was born on January 15, 1980, and we named her after Ardell's mom. When Leah was two weeks old, she took her first plane ride: Ardell and the girls moved to Medicine Hat for the rest of the hockey season, and it was their turn to commute. Leah was a seasoned traveller by the time she was three months old.

Leah has always been very independent, and she taught herself to read through sheer determination. When she was only five, she'd sit down with a *Reader's Digest* or a newspaper in her hand and tell us not to bother her because she was "reading." Andra was a great reader and we thought that Leah was just imitating her big sister. We couldn't believe it when she called us over one day and said, "I want to read you something." And she did!

When we were living in Denver, Andra and Leah were in a Christmas fashion show, modelling fancy party dresses. They were supposed to walk on to the stage, twirl around, curtsy and exit stage left. All went well, but when the girls curtsied, Leah heard the applause, so she twirled again. More applause. She twirled some more. She's a born entertainer—just like her daddy. Leah was almost two then, and she knew what she liked! Andra eventually had to lead her off stage, and although she didn't leave willingly, her big sister finally convinced her to wave goodbye to her adoring audience.

Leah is now seven and, like her grandpa Lorne, you can tell how happy she is by the sparkle in her eyes. She's got a smile that lights up her whole face and a grin that can brighten anyone's day.

Then, a new city, a new team, another baby. We were three for three! Barrett James made his appearance amid much hoopla on October 18, 1982. This was the first of our children to be born "at home," and the Foothills Hospital saw a steady stream of adoring family for our first son. People naturally assume that we want him to grow up to be a hockey player, "just like dad," but BJ seems to have other ideas. I overhead him tell his poppie the other day that he wanted to be a doctor (probably his mother's influence). However, Barrett does enjoy playing road hockey, and he knows how to stick with the winners. After our Stanley Cup finals last year, Barrett asked if I wanted to play hockey with him. He handed me a stick and said, "You be the Calgary Flames, Dad, and I'll be the Montreal Canadiens." I wondered why he wanted to be a Canadien instead of a Flame, and his reply put me in my place. "Well, Dad, you guys won the Campbell Cup, but the Montreal guys won the Stanley Cup." And they say kids don't know what's going on. Not bad for a three-and-a-half year old.

And then there were four: our second son, Graham Daniel, was born on March 12, 1987. The kids had waited for his arrival for what seemed to them like years. They sat anxiously in Ardell's hospital room with their grandma for word of a baby brother or sister. The girls just wanted a baby; they didn't care whether it was a sister of a brother. But Barrett desperately wanted the baby to be a boy. Ardell had explained to him that as long as the baby was healthy, it didn't really matter if it was a boy or a girl. "Yes, Mommy, I understand," he replied. "As long as it's a healthy brother."

I had promised the kids to come and give them the news as soon as the baby was born. Ardell's nurse, Penny, believes that the birth of a new baby is a family event and suggested that we bring the kids into the recovery room. So Graham was less than an hour old when he met his big brother and sisters. And it was one of the most touching family moments we'll ever share. Andra, Leah and Barrett all think of Graham as their special responsibility: Andra holds and cuddles him; Leah was rewarded with his first smile and can always make him laugh; and BJ sings lullabies and smothers him with kisses.

We were a little concerned about what Barrett's reaction to his new baby brother would be. After all, he was the youngest and the only boy and had been "crown prince" for four years. But he's graciously moved over and now shares the title with Graham.

How we've changed! With our first baby, nothing was allowed to interrupt her schedule. Our timetable revolved around Andra: If we had to go out at 1 p.m. and Andra was still napping, we'd wait unto she woke up before leaving. Ten years later, Graham's schedule rotates around swimming lessons, jazz classes, tumbling competitions or whatever the gang is doing. As a matter of fact, he really should get a lot of credit for allowing us to write this book! Every man tries to be a good father, but it's a tough job without a great mother to work with. And as far as I'm concerned, Ardell really is the world's best mother. She bears a lot of the responsibility for our family, especially during the hockey season, when I'm on the road. Often Ardell ends up at Christmas concerts or parents' days alone, and I'm sure that sometimes she feels like a single parent. She has to deal with the everyday trials and tribulations of raising the kids, and just when the daily schedule is established, I'll come home from a road trip, and the regular routine goes all out of whack. I'm not saying I spoil the kids, but after being away for an average of seventeen days a month during the hockey season, I tend to come home and bend the rules a little more than I would if I were there all the time. Ardell makes a point of being home when the kids are, even though she's involved with a number of charities and works with the school on a regular basis. Her university training in early childhood education has certainly been put to good use with our four.

Ardell does have help though. Her sister, Joanne, lives with us and makes life easier for us all. She's our "major domo," and we like to tease her that when she gives orders, we snap to attention. But we know we couldn't do without her. It's reassuring to know that Ardell has someone to count on and be with while I'm on the road: With four kids going three different ways, the two of them are kept running. Joanne is the greatest cook in the world, and often I've seen Leah and Barrett perched on the counter, helping her make her famous cheesecake. She can see the funny side of anything, is a master at giving me a bad time and fills our house with laughter.

Having gone full circle and coming home to Calgary has reaffirmed our belief in the importance of the extended family. Our children are growing up with the luxury of having grandparents, aunts, uncles and cousins nearby. They're part of our everyday life. Leah and Barrett share a garden with Uncle Ken; the cousins get together and have lip-sync contests; and it feels natural to the kids when Grandma and Poppie stay with them when Ardell and I go away for a few days.

Life as the child of a professional athlete can be tough. Our kids sometimes deal with situations that call for an understanding beyond their years. We don't try to shelter our children from public life; it's part of my job, and we all must learn to deal with the good and the bad aspects of it. It's hard to teach the kids that they have to separate the "Lanny McDonald" being talked about in the paper or at school from the man who comes through the door after work. It's hard for them not to feel hurt when someone criticizes their daddy, and it can be difficult for them not to get swelled heads when things are going well. But the kids must realize they have their own value and that people like them for what *they* are, not because of who their daddy is. Living in the country and being part of the Springbank community help. We attend many of the community events, and we know everyone in the area. To most, I'm just another neighbour who has a bunch of kids and happens to play hockey on the side. But keeping our lives as normal as possible is something that we always have to work at.

When we're in Calgary, we're busy with hockey games, charity functions, commercials, speaking engagements and the myriad commitments that go with the game. I know how much an autograph meant to me as a youngster, and I make a supreme effort not only to sign each scrap of paper, but to talk to each fan. Our kids sometimes find it hard to accept people asking for autographs during family excursions; however, they also know that if Madonna were at the next table, they'd want to run up and get her autograph.

But once we're at the lake for the summer, it's family time. It's there that we are able to leave hockey and the public arena behind us. It's there that we have the chance to be a "normal" family, hiking in the mornings, waterskiing, windsurfing, bicycling to the store, playing Yahtzee and Rummy-o during rainstorms and spending evenings in front of a beach fire. If we go to the show, we go together. If we go out for supper, it's to a family restaurant. It's a great time to make up for some of those days during the winter when hockey keeps me away from home. The summers belong to us.

When we were traded to Calgary, we decided to live in the country. Initially, Ardell wasn't sure she could live more than three blocks from a convenience store, but we wouldn't move now for the world. Waking up every morning to the sun shining on the Rocky Mountains is a great way to start your day, and we love having that little bit of space of our own. Ardell teases me that my favourite thing to do is to ride the garden tractor and act like a farmer.

We're a very close family, and it's great to be met at the door with hugs and kisses, whether you've been gone ten days or just a few hours. The kids are very understanding of hockey life and realize that road trips are part of that life. I make a point of spending a little time with each one before I leave, and I call home every day when I'm gone. The kids are very supportive of my career, and sometimes when we've lost a big game, I'll come home and find strung across the foyer a "Sorry you lost, Daddy" poster. And during our Stanley Cup final playoffs, they made a different "good luck" poster for every game. Leah often says, as I'm going out the door, "Give 'em hell, Daddy," repeating what she had heard others say. The kids' first question the morning after a game is "Who won?" Their second question is "Who scored?" They're always interested to know if Daddy put one in the net.

Honesty is a primary in our home, and we've taught the kids never to be afraid to tell us anything. They know that, if there's a problem, we'll work it out together. Bedtime is especially important; it's time not only for reading a story and saying prayers but for talking over the day. Children need a private time with their parents to talk about things that are important to them, and knowing how to listen is an essential part of being a parent. I guess we sometimes get carried away thinking our kids can do no wrong, but I must admit there are times when discipline becomes necessary. We have certain rules and regulations in our home, and we feel that children not only need but want those sorts of guidelines.

I hope that 20 years from now, we'll be able to look back and say we did the right thing, that we were good parents. We feel blessed to have our four children, and we realize that, although hockey is important, there's more to life than hockey. Hockey means nothing if we fail as parents. To balance our professional and personal lives takes a whole lot of love and understanding.

Ardell keeps us all on an even keel. She's the one who makes sure we keep things in perspective during the good times; she's the one who restores our confidence and faith during the bad times. Ardell always encourages me, but she's also able to give me a kick in the butt when I feel sorry for myself and think things aren't going my way. More than anything, she's taught me how to deal with life's ups and downs. She's the one I talk to when something is bothering me. I trust her judgement completely, especially her perceptions of people. She's my confidante, my advisor and my conscience. She's more than my wife: She's the best mother any kids could have; she's the love of my life and my best friend.

So Billy Clement, "I'd like to thank Ardell and the kids."

20

OLD
McDONALD

I'm getting old, and it isn't easy. I just turned thirty-four, which is young in most careers, but in professional hockey it's considered old. And I'd be lying if I said there isn't a lot of pain involved.

Sometimes, it's tough to accept your age, to realize that your career is nearing the end. A wise friend and ex-teammate of mine, Mike Eaves, had the best description I've heard of a hockey player's career. He said you come into the league and try to find your place. Then, after a few years, you've found that place, you've established your spot and you finally belong. And just as you're feeling comfortable about belonging, it's all over.

It doesn't matter whether your career lasts one year or fourteen years, you can't believe how fast it goes. You know in your own mind that you can still play and do the job the way you always have, but other people are questioning whether you still have the ability, whether your legs are strong enough, whether you're still fast enough. They question everything once you hit a certain age, and the questions become a part of your daily life.

Still, you've played at a certain level for most of your career, and when you feel your chance to play is taken away from you prematurely, it's difficult to accept. If the willingness isn't there, it's one thing. But if you're just not getting the ice time, it's another, and you have to learn to deal with that.

The saddest part of nearing the end is the politics involved. The minute you turn thirty, people begin to write you off. It doesn't matter what you've accomplished in the past, you're not expected to do it anymore. It's funny, one season you can set a league record for playing the most games in a year and scoring 11 goals in the playoffs. Then, just a few months later, people are saying you're too old to play.

Although Bob Johnson and I got along, we did have our differences. There were times when I thought he considered me a threat: Not to his coaching career, but in the dressing room. I've never done anything to undermine his coaching or to hurt the hockey club, and I never would. My suggestions have always been given for the benefit of the club.

CJ (for Coach Johnson) has an intelligent hockey mind. He knows the game inside out and works extremely hard at his job; and with his college coaching background, he stresses the technical side of the game. Even though his record speaks for itself, I sincerely believe that the Flames' success could have been even greater if Bob had placed more emphasis on encouragement and motivation. I know it's our job but even professional athletes need a pat on the back once in a while.

To be honest, I dread to think of not playing hockey, because I've learned so much about life, about friendships, about the game. I've had a chance to see the game from all sides: Playing in Toronto for the team I cheered for as a kid; playing in Colorado with a franchise fighting for survival; playing in Calgary and enjoying the rise of the Flames as an NHL power. I guess you could say it's enough to write a book about.

After 14 years, you become accustomed to this way of life, so much so that you can't picture what it would be like away from hockey. People say it's glamorous, but it's not; it's hard work. It means being on the road away from home, feeling pressure, being subjected to public scrutiny. But it's my life, and I wouldn't change it for the world. As long as I can remember I've been waking up and going to the rink in the morning. You get used to being around the guys, sharing good times and bad, helping each other through the terrible times, feeling great when things are going well. I think what I'll miss most is the camaraderie on a hockey team.

Each day brings me closer to retirement. I don't now exactly when that last day will be, but I plan to play my fifteenth season and then evaluate the situation. I'm leaving my options open. I think I'll know when the time is right to quit. If anyone had told me I'd play 14 years in the NHL, I would have said they had the wrong guy. As a dream, I couldn't have asked for anything more.

Now, as I look back, the hardest part of my career may also have been the most beneficial. If anything, my difficult start in Toronto made me appreciate the good years all the more. Going into the league, I knew there would be an apprenticeship; I just didn't realize it would take more than two years. As much as I struggled in Toronto, I don't think I would want to change the beginnings. Those were tough years, but not as hard as the years at the end.

There are indications all around the league that I'm

an oldtimer. Nine of the current general managers are guys I played against. I've played with or against seven of the coaches in their playing days. I've tried to rationalize it, saying that I caught them at the end of their playing careers. But then there's the fact that, out of the 450 players in the league, only four—Marcel Dionne, Larry Robinson, Billy Smith and Gilles Meloche—have been there longer than I have.

With age comes pain. Some of it's mental. Some of it's physical. I've always prided myself on playing physical hockey; it was the way I had to play to survive. In the early days, I'd get hit, and feel it, but the pain would go away. In the last couple of years, I'll get hit and it doesn't go away; it becomes second nature to play with pain. It becomes mind over matter; a question of just how badly you want to play.

I've spent a lot of time talking to Doug Risebrough during the past few years. As the two oldest members of the Flames, both of us are placed in leadership roles, and we both have had to endure major injuries in our careers. While our bodies don't cooperate the way they once did, neither of us has lost the most important characteristic an athlete can have: That willingness to compete. That's what kept us going this long. It's funny how the game works. You never stop thinking, you never stop believing that tomorrow will be the best day yet. That's always been my attitude.

I guess there are two ways you can approach the end of your career. One is to say it's ending too soon. The other is to say, I've had a pretty damn good career. But no matter which one you choose, it doesn't make the process any easier.

Someone asked me not long ago if I'd been hearing hints that I should be thinking of retiring. Actually, I haven't heard a thing. But I will say that I feel the pressure from within. When I look at my stats, naturally I'm disappointed. My playing time has decreased from year to year. The more ice time you have, the more confidence you gain. The more confident you are, the more scoring chances you get. It's a snowball effect.

The transition is difficult. The hardest part is accepting your changing role as a player. You still have dreams, and you don't like to see them taken away. I need 21 goals to reach 500 and 35 points to reach 1000. But most of all, I still want to win the Stanley Cup. I hope that those goals are within reach, but I've never sacrificed team goals for my personal ones, and after 14 years, I sure won't start now. Deep down, I feel I can play this season and play effectively. My self-perception is important, and I won't have trouble being honest, especially with the kind of pressure I put on myself. I want to walk away with grace and dignity.

If there is an ultimate way to finish a career, Jean Beliveau did it. He went out exactly the way he played: successfully, with skills and pride intact. In his last season, he played well; the Montreal Canadiens won the Stanley Cup and he retired, although he certainly had enough left to continue playing. That's the dream way to finish.

Still, this career has been a dream come true. As a family, we've worked awfully hard at it. We've had all kinds of help from all kinds of people, but there's a part of your life you can enjoy only when you retire from the game. I don't look forward to retirement, but I do look forward to the day I'll get to spend more time with Ardell and the kids.

I've had a great introduction to the business world through the companies I've been associated with, and I'd like to continue those relationships.

But most of all, I'd like to remain in hockey, the profession that has been my life and that I've loved so much. When my playing days are over, I hope that people will look back and respect me as Lanny Mc-

Donald, the man, and not only as Lanny McDonald, the hockey player.

You can prepare for the future. It's the present that's difficult. The biggest problem with a career in professional sports is that it ends before you're ready. Sometimes I wish it would never end.

There's a saying in pro hockey: "You're only as good as your last shift." Damn, I hope it's a great one!!

21

PS: AFTERTHOUGHTS

In the course of a career, many things happen that you don't think about until something— or someone— jogs your memory. That's what this chapter is about. We spent hours laughing over memories that seemed both so long ago and as recent as yesterday. This chapter is a grab-bag of those stories and thoughts and memories. It's like sitting around with old buddies having a cool one...

Did I tell you about the time when...

The Leafs were playing the Canadiens, and we had a three on two. I was carrying the puck, and it somehow got caught up in my skates. I looked down to find it, got it back up on my stick and at the last second, saw Larry Robinson cruising in on my radar. I shovelled the puck through his legs to Sittler, and that's the last thing I remember. The truck hit me, square on! I crawled over to the bench and tried to get into the players box, but no one would open the gate. Darryl scored, and on his way back, picked me up and pointed me in the right direction. I had been trying to get into the Canadiens' box instead of my own. What a way to learn to keep your head up!

How about the night we were playing the Islanders.... Darryl and I were killing a penalty during a game with the Islanders. I stole the puck from Potvin and headed back up the ice. I cut toward the centre, and all of a sudden, train #9, Clark Gillies, hit me so hard that my helmet popped off. I landed on my right shoulder, slamming my ear into the ice. I remember lying there and Borje Salming being the first guy to reach me. I couldn't see him, but I could hear him. "Mackie, Mackie, talk to me." I tried to talk, but nothing was working. Borje turned to the rest of the team and said, "I think he's dead!" Joe Sgro, the trainer, came out and asked me where it hurt. It would have been easier to tell to tell him where it didn't hurt! I had separated both shoulders; I had a concussion, and it took 26 stitches to sew my ear back on. I had been hit by the Gilles Railroad! And how could I forget that....

Barry Beck and I have always had a friendly rivalry on the ice. While I was playing with Colorado and he was with the Rangers, it intensified somewhat. It was nothing for the two of us to run each other five or six times in a game, seeing who could knock the other one down first. Since Barry outweighed me by some 30 pounds, you can guess who usually won! I finally accomplished my mission during a game in New York by setting him on his butt. Later in that same game, I was breaking wide and cutting toward their net about 10 feet from the boards when I felt myself being lifted and muscled into the corner. I hit the boards right where the

Zamboni comes out, and the wall gave way. The doors hadn't been locked properly, and they sprung open. There was I, stumbling down the runway with a stunned look on my face. The whistle blew. I skated back onto the ice; Beck was standing about 25 feet away from me. I skated right up to him, and a hush fell over the crowd. Everyone thought we were going to fight: skinny little me against big, bad Bubba Beck. But I was smarter than that; I told him, "Next time, Bubba, can you put a little something into it?" Then with a smirk, I skated away. When I got back to the bench, the guys wanted to know what I'd said to Beck. I figured I'd play it to the hilt and told them that I'd threatened to fight it out with him if he ever tried that again. They laughed, knowing there were two chances of me challenging Barry: slim and none.

I guess I have to admit, it hasn't only been other teams that have caused me pain....

In practice one time with the Maple Leafs, I shot the puck past goalie Wayne Thomas. It hit the crossbar and came out the other side, smashing into my forehead and cutting me for six stitches. It's pretty embarrassing to try coming up with a good story to explain the cut on your face when 20 guys in practice know the truth!

And then there was the time I jumped over the boards at the Calgary Corral, ready to take a shift on the ice. My linemate, Jamie Hislop, was going out at the same time and our skates locked in mid jump, sending us both flying. He landed on his knees, but I did a one-point landing— flat on my back. It knocked the wind completely out me, and I crawled back into the box. I never did play that shift.

Pressure really builds during the season, and sometimes a little humour can relieve the tension....

During a Flames-Whalers game, we were leading, and their tough guy, Archie Henderson, wanted to get his team going; he was really trying to stir something up.

After our captain, Phil Russell, had rubbed him out in the corner, Archie turned to Rusty and said, "D'ya wanna go, Russell?" (meaning "do you want to fight?"). Rusty turned to him and said in his slow drawl, "Well, if it's all the same to you, Archie, no thanks." Everybody cracked up. The two combatants grinned and skated away.

Nick Fotiu is your classic prankster in the dressing room, and one of his favourite tricks is to put a layer of vaseline between the folds of the shower towels. One day, no one had reacted to his antics, so Nick asked Bearcat what the scoop was. Why hadn't anybody complained about the towels? "What towels?" asked Bearcat. "The ones that were stacked by the showers," explained Nick. Bearcat started to laugh. "Those were the towels I sent to the Vancouver Canucks dressing room!"

The Flames' players always had a rule against smoking and fined anyone who broke it. A certain player— who shall remain nameless (right, Baxie?)—used to sneak into the bathroom for the odd cigarette, and although he was caught on numerous occasions, he never seemed to cough up the fine money. One day, smoke was billowing over the top of a cubicle door, and Riser and Pep sounded the alarm, running through the dressing room yelling, "Fire, fire!" They grabbed a garbage can—a big one that appeared out of nowhere and, to our surprise, was filled with water—and threw it on the smouldering fire. The way they tell the story, they saved all our lives. But Baxie was rather upset, and even though the cigarette had been doused, the air was still blue.

I have a collection of "it-was-so-bad" stories, too....

Brian Glennie and I were teammates on the Leafs and had been asked to do a commercial together. We figured it would take a couple of hours or so. After all, how hard can it be to say a few lines. We found out real soon. Well, maybe not so soon. We spent more than eight hours trying to get enough usable footage for a 30-second commercial. We were so bad that we ended up looking funny, and they closed the spot with an out-take. The best part is that we must have done something right. The commercial, which was supposed to run for 13 weeks, ran for 78! Meow!

How about the time I caught a fish this big....

After the Canada Cup in 1976, Jim Gregory gave Darryl and me a few days off from the Leafs training camp, and we thought we'd treat our wives to a little holiday. Wendy and Ardell wanted to go to Florida, but Darryl thought a fishing trip up north would be relaxing—just what we needed after an intensive series. We went fishing. The camp was in the middle of nowhere; the girls weren't too impressed. It was cold, it rained, and all I caught was a cold and a clam. Darryl always caught his daily limit and thought it was great fun, but I have to tell you, that's the last time he was in charge of planning a vacation!

And people say the darnedest things....

The fans of the Rockies—although there weren't many of them—were the best. McNichols Arena held 16,000 people, but the Rockies were lucky to have 5000 at a game. I must say, though, that those 5000 fans could make as much noise as another full house in the league. But not everyone in Denver was a fan. I remember one of our neighbours asking Andra what her daddy did. Andra told him that daddy played hockey. The neighbour said, "No, what does he do for a living?"

Receiving the Colorado Athlete of the Year award was very special to me because hockey was new in that city and considerably less important than football, basketball and soccer. The local television stations included the Rockies scores during the sportscast, but only after the highlights of the local high-school basketball games.

I always admired Gordie Howe and found him to be

the gentleman everyone said he was, but my first encounter with him was less than friendly. In a game against Hartford, I checked his son, Mark, into the boards. Heading back up the ice, Gordie's "atomic elbow" came out of nowhere and hit me right in the chops. Smoothly, Gordie skated by and said, "Don't ever do that again." I didn't... at least, not while Gordie was around.

My first game in the Boston Gardens was against the burly Bruins. We were in the faceoff circle, and I was lined up against Wayne Cashman. Just before the puck was dropped, Cashman stomped on the blade of my stick and broke it. He looked at me and said, "What are you going to do about it, kid?" I looked him right in the eye and said, "Guess I'll go get another stick." I may have been young, but I wasn't stupid. I knew how to handle myself with the tough guys in the league.

You meet the greatest people playing hockey....

Sometimes you can't remember the first time you met someone because it feels like you've been friends all your life. It was like that for me with Rick Sutcliffe. When Ardell and I were first married, the Leafs scheduled a Sunday road game almost every week, and Rick made a point of taking Ardell and Inge Turnball out for brunch on each of those road-game Sundays. When I was traded to Colorado, Rick rearranged his life so that he could stay at our house with Ardell, Andra and Lucille, making sure that they were well taken care of while I was gone. Rick's the kind of guy who always is around then you need him the most. Even though "Buddy Buddy" is a Torontonian and claims to have a maple leaf tattooed on his behind, Rick spends every Christmas with us in Calgary, and it's rumoured that he's even cheered for the Flames once or twice.

Everyone thinks that my singing and dancing career originated with the Apollo muffler ads, but it really started way back in Toronto. Rick owned a wine bar called

Grapes, and it was a favourite spot for Leaf parties. I remember one New Year's Eve when the Good Brothers were entertaining at Grapes, and they called me up on the stage to sing "Alberta Bound" (Ardell says it didn't take much urging). What they didn't realize was that I only knew the chorus, but I belted that part out with all my heart— right through the whole song! Bruce, Brian and Larry are great guys, but they never did ask me to tour with them, and I guess I can understand why.

The Flames' wives were putting together their first annual charity dinner and fashion show and had the bright idea that the models should include the players and their children, as well as the wives and girlfriends. Mike Eaves volunteered to choreograph a lip-sync group, the Imitations, patterned after the Temptations. His idea was to open the formal-wear segment with the song "My Girl," which our group, dressed in tuxedos, would sing while dancing to the music. The first practice was planned to last an hour. Four hours later, we were still swinging when Mike wanted us to be swaying. I've never seen such good-natured patience from anybody. He'd take each one of us aside and walk us through the steps, saying, "Just feel the music." Poor Mike really had his work cut out with me; at one point, I think he wished he could run to the store and get some rhythm for me. Mike started Joel Otto on his road to stardom, though. When the music started and the spotlight came on, Joel became the ultimate showman, and his performance was met with screams that recalled Beatlemania. Mike had to count the rest of us through the number. Boz, Perry, and Mike looked like the real thing, but I think I turned out to be the comic relief.

In 1977 I was asked for the first time to participate in "Superstars." A collection of sportsmen from different fields was brought together to compete in a series of events like bike riding, swimming, tennis, rowing, soccer kick, weight lifting and running. It gave me a chance to meet a number of people I wouldn't normally meet, like: Brian Budd, a great all-round athlete who made the rest of us compete for second place; Dave Cutler, one of the funniest men I've ever met and one who has a story for every occasion; Tony Gabriel, the elder statesman of the CFL; Mark McKoy, who made the rest of us look like we were walking in the running events; Rocky DiPietro, the original "Rocky"; Ken Clark, one of the finest punters ever; and Gaetan Boucher, Canada's Olympic speedskating medalist.

Ready or not....

When I was with the Leafs, Willy Brossart played defence, and there was a stretch of about seven or eight games where he had been warming the bench, dressed but not playing. We were playing in Minnesota and losing badly. Sitting in his usual spot at the end of the bench, Willy loosened his skates and bribed the stick boy to sneak him some popcorn. Willy hadn't even finished his snack when Red Kelly yelled, "Brossart, you're up." Without missing a beat Willy jumped over the boards, popcorn flying everywhere. During his shift, we weren't sure if Willy was just tripping over his laces or if he really was blocking shots. Grinning from ear to ear, he arrived back at the bench to cheers from the guys but a stiff fine from the Leafs.

Sometimes the call to duty is a double-edged compliment. Reggie Lemelin became ill before a game and was sent home. His back-up, Marc D'Amour, better known as Shaky, was in the nets. We were part way through the third period of a game against the Devils, and Shaky was suffering from a bout of dehydration. The coach approached Colin Patterson, a left winger who likes pretending he's a major-league goalie in practice, and asked if he was ready to replace Shaky if need be. As it turned out, Shaky finished the game, but Colin—the Rodney Dangerfield of the Flames—still wonders if CJ really thought he was the player least likely to be missed on the bench or if he, in fact, was the next best thing to a real goalie.

O.K. Just one Tiger story for the road....

The Leafs were in the playoffs when Tiger and Dave Hutchison of the Kings got in a stick-swinging incident. The league suspended Tiger for the first five games of the following regular season, and Tiger wrote a letter of protest to Brian O'Neill, vice-president of the NHL. In training camp of the following year, Tiger was complaining in the dressing room that Mr. O'Neill hadn't even had the decency to reply to his letter. Jim McKenny piped up, "Tiger, did you ever think that maybe your crayon smudged?"

And one last thing to mention....

After the Stanley Cup playoffs in 1986, Calgary had a "Thank-You-Flames" parade. We drove to the arena that morning to get the bus that was taking the team to the start of the parade. At first, there was no one along the route, and we chuckled, thinking about how it would feel to give a parade and have nobody show up. But as the parade wound its way down 9th Avenue, the crowd seemed to grow. By the time we reached the city centre, the streets were jammed. The police estimated the crowd at more than 125,000 and then we realized just how completely the City of Calgary was behind us, even though we'd lost the final series. I hope that before my hockey-playing days are over, we get a chance to ride down that same street again— this time with the Stanley Cup.

PPS (June, 1987)
Before last season, I needed 35 goals to reach 500. I felt that was within range especially after scoring two goals in the opening game of the 86/87 season. Instead, I wound up with a knee injury for four weeks, a reinjury of the same knee and a needless three-game suspension,

none of which I could do anything about and all of which meant that my season kept being put on hold. Those aren't excuses, just the circumstances. Naturally, I'd like to have scored more. It just didn't happen—this time.

I can't tell you how much I'm looking forward to training camp. Oldtime hockey is here again. Sounds like we're going to have some fun!

INDEX

A NOTE ON STEVE SIMMONS

Steve Simmons has written about hockey for four Canadian newspapers, several magazines and is a regular contributor to *The Hockey News*. A staff sports writer with *The Toronto Sun*, Simmons admits a preference for writing about hockey and boxing, two sports that sometimes have a lot in common. This is his second book. His first, *On Fire: The Dramatic Rise of the Calgary Flames*, co-written with Eric Duhatschek, was published in 1986. Simmons covered the Calgary Flames for seven years. Now making his home in Thornhill, Ontario, Simmons, 31, lives with his wife, Sheila, and son Jeffrey.